THE WINGS *of* *the* MORNING

FOURTH WATCH PRAYER

THE WINGS *of* *the* MORNING

FOURTH WATCH PRAYER

A Face to Face Appearance from Jesus During 3am Morning Prayer

DAVID E. TAYLOR

© Copyright 2020 – David E. Taylor

All rights reserved. This book is protected by the copyright laws of the United States of America. This book may not be copied or reprinted for commercial gain or profit. The use of short quotations or occasional page copying for personal or group study is permitted and encouraged. Permission will be granted upon request. Unless otherwise identified, Scripture quotations are from the King James Bible Version. All rights reserved. Please note that the publishing style capitalizes certain pronouns in scripture that refer to the Father, Son, and Holy Spirit, and may differ from some publishers' styles.

Due to the revelatory nature of these encounters and because of the author's desire to preserve a very intimate and personal reading experience, editorial license was taken to maintain the emotional impact of the stories as they were told.

KINGDOM OF GOD GLOBAL CHURCH
20320 Superior Rd
Taylor, MI 48180

For more information on ordering products (books, CDs, DVDs, etc.) from David E. Taylor, and for information on the next Miracles in America Crusades happening around the world, call 877-843-4567.

Or visit on the Internet: www.kingdomofgodglobalchurch.org

ISBN 13: 978-1-64815-021-0

For Worldwide Distribution, Printed in the U.S.A.

Dedication

*To Jesus, my Best Friend who is
the very reason for my being,
who has stood with me through
the darkest times of my life.
To the person of the Holy Spirit,
Who is also my Friend and closest companion.*

Table of Contents

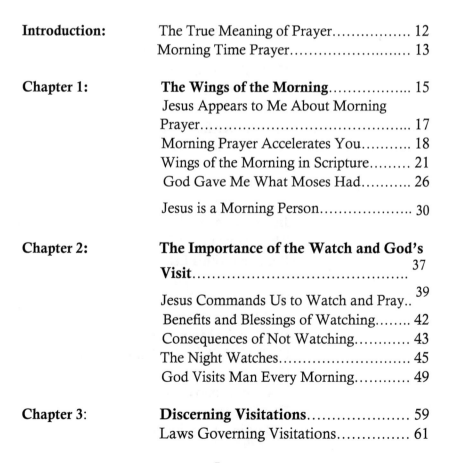

Introduction:	The True Meaning of Prayer.................. 12
	Morning Time Prayer.......................... 13
Chapter 1:	**The Wings of the Morning**.................. 15
	Jesus Appears to Me About Morning Prayer... 17
	Morning Prayer Accelerates You........... 18
	Wings of the Morning in Scripture......... 21
	God Gave Me What Moses Had.......... 26
	Jesus is a Morning Person.................... 30
Chapter 2:	**The Importance of the Watch and God's Visit**... 37
	Jesus Commands Us to Watch and Pray.. 39
	Benefits and Blessings of Watching........ 42
	Consequences of Not Watching............ 43
	The Night Watches........................... 45
	God Visits Man Every Morning........... 49
Chapter 3:	**Discerning Visitations**..................... 59
	Laws Governing Visitations............... 61

	Knowing the Time of Your Visitation...... 62
	The Enemy Comes if You Miss Your Visitation.. 65
Chapter 4:	**Forty Benefits of Fourth Watch Prayer**....73
	Rewards of Morning Time Visitation..75
Chapter 5:	**The Mercies of Fourth Watch**................ 79
	New Mercies Belong to Your Peace........ 81
	The Sure Mercies of David....................82
	How I Received the Covenant............... 83
Chapter 6:	**God Awakens You in the Morning**..... 97
	God Awakens for You........................ 98
	Coming Before the Lord at Other Times of the Day......................101
	He Wakes You Up Morning by Morning..102
Chapter 7:	**Your Latter End Greatly Increases**........... 105
	Fourth Watch Prayer Increases You.......... 107
Chapter 8:	**The Ear and Tongue of the Learned**..........111
	God Gives You the Ear of the Learned In the Morning......................................113
	The Learned Ear Closes at Dawn.............114
	Speaking with a Learned Tongue.............118
Chapter 9:	**What Happens in the Morning**................ 121
	You Receive a Prophetic Word in the Morning..............................123
	God's Early Morning Pattern...................125
	God Changes Your Name.......................128
	You Come into the Inheritance of The Fathers..135
	A Blessing is Pronounced on You............ 137

	Joy Comes in the Morning................ 139
	Plants Grow in the Morning...............143
	God Brings Justice to Light.................151
	God Fights for You...........................158
Chapter 10:	**The Womb of the Morning**.................157
	Cherished in the Womb of the Morning..163
	Why Your Love Gets Cold...................165
Chapter 11:	**Royal Power of a Prince**.................... 171
	Morning Prayer Makes You a Prince.... 173
	You are a King and a Priest................ 174
	The Making of a Prince.....................176
	Establishing the Stronghold of Peace......179
Chapter 12:	**Power from God**............................. 183
	You See God's Power in the Morning.....195
	Virtue is Restored in the Fourth Watch... 188
	Coming into Power with God...............192
	Power with Men is Released in the Morning...200
Chapter 13:	**Glory in the Morning**.......................205
	Coming into Your Glory During Fourth Watch....................................207
	You See God's Glory in the Morning..... 209
	God's Glory vs Your Glory................. 213
Chapter 14:	**History and Mysteries of Fourth Watch Prayer** 219
	God Commands the Morning.............. 221
	Discernment to Choose a Staff............. 222
	Mysteries of Fourth Watch Prayer......... 225

INTRODUCTION

  I want to share with you how important morning prayer is to your life and ministry. This is just one of the prayer books the Lord commissioned me to write. A few generations ago, the Body of Christ was a praying church, but that has changed in this generation as the love of many has grown cold. Prayer is a very important part of seeing the promises of God manifest in the natural realm, however, it is constantly declining in our day. Several years ago, there were very strong prayer movements all over America, but most of them have died out. Even nations known for prayer, like South Korea, have stopped praying like they used to because of prosperity and wealth.

  With the Prayer Series I am launching a major prayer movement will be awakened. Prayer kings will be raised up all over this nation who will intercede, prevail, and travail until a Glory revival breaks out across the land. A new move is on the scene and it will take prayer to fully birth it! It is not a move of the Holy Ghost anointing, gifts, or ministry gifts, it is a Glory Move where God Himself, Jesus, and the Holy Spirit manifest on earth to reap the end-time harvest. Isaiah spoke about this new move,

  "Arise, shine; for thy light is come, and the glory of the LORD is risen upon thee. For, behold, the darkness shall cover the earth, and gross darkness the people: but the LORD shall arise upon thee, and his glory shall be

seen upon thee. And the Gentiles shall come to thy light, and kings to the brightness of thy rising," (Isaiah 60:1-3).

This is a move where the Glory of God will rise and be seen upon us! For that to happen, God said we must **"Arise, shine ..."** What does it mean to arise? It means to wake up from the spiritual lethargy and slumber that has engulfed the church! To arise means to wake up early in the morning, meet with, and fellowship with the Lord and that is the essence of this book you are holding in your hands! To arise means to rouse yourself from slumber and PRAY.

"Wherefore he saith, Awake thou that sleepest, and arise from the dead, and Christ shall give thee light," (Ephesians 5:14).

In this hour the Lord is stirring the Body of Christ to rise and pray! *"Therefore let us not sleep, as do others; but let us watch and be sober,"* (1 Thessalonians 5:6). Prayer is the foundation for all revivals that have ever hit the earth. You cannot have revival without prayer, it is the key. All major moves of God were birthed by intense prayer. Through these books, a major prayer revival will sweep all over America and the nations of the world.

The True Meaning of Prayer
True Prayer is Connection with God

This book is about morning prayer therefore, I must explain what true prayer is. The core meaning of prayer is fellowship with God. Prayer is not a monologue it is a dialogue. It is you and God communing and talking with each other. In prayer, God meets with you and you both talk to each other. When God commissioned Moses to build a tabernacle for Him to dwell with the children of Israel He said, **"And there I will meet with thee, and I will commune with thee from above the mercy seat..."** (Exodus 25:22). Prayer is communion with God – both of you communicating. Prayer is boring if all you do is shout and cry aloud to the Lord and get no response. True prayer takes place when you make connection with God.

Introduction

Prayer is not just you talking to God and making requests, it is also fellowshipping with Him. Many people pray religiously, but they don't fellowship and commune with the Lord. They are like the Pharisees that Jesus had to rebuke for reducing prayer to a pretentious religious exercise. Jesus described them as hypocrites who *"... love to pray standing in the synagogues and in the corners of the streets, that they may be seen of men. Verily I say unto you, They have their reward,"* (Matthew 6:5). You see, prayer will be boring if it is not done out of love. It is the relationship that keeps your heart warm and makes you want to rush to go pray! It is the relationship that makes you stay in prayer for hours.

Religion makes prayer hard and tedious. I believe prayer becomes boring when it becomes religious. You know your prayer life becomes a religious exercise when you say *"Ahh, I've got to pray again today... Oh, how long before I will be done praying?"* You pray and it is not exciting – it's supposed to be exciting! Feeling the Holy Spirit surge through you as you pray is exciting. I do know about agonizing or travailing prayer, but that is for certain reasons and seasons. Normal prayer is supposed to be refreshing, you should be excited to get up and run to your room to go be with God. Just this morning, I ran to my place of prayer to be with the Lord. He woke me up at 3:33 a.m. and before I knew it, the sun was up and tears were flowing down my face as I communed and fellowshipped intimately and intensely with Him. I am consistent in my prayer life because I focus on intimacy. I always want to be around God and morning time prayer is so important to me. I pray it will become important to you too!

Morning Time Prayer

I need you to understand that the revelation I am sharing with you and a lot of the other revelations I have received over the years did not come to me because I went to seminary school. Although I have been taught and trained by some of the best men of God around the world, and I have spent countless hours meditating and studying the word for 30 years, the revelations I have received came directly from Jesus Christ. He took me on as a personal disciple and taught me through face to face appearances.

THE WINGS OF THE MORNING

The visitations I am referring to have been verified by major fathers around the world because they started having visitations from the Lord after they got connected with my life and ministry. When they hear me teach the revelations the Lord taught me, they say, *"David, you couldn't have gotten this revelation in a theological school. This word you are teaching is so ancient relevant and accurate. Jesus had to appear to you to give you these revelations."* I am so humbled by these confirmations from the fathers. Like Paul the Apostle I can say,

*"But I certify you, brethren, that the gospel which was preached of me is not after man. **For I neither received it of man, neither was I taught it, but by the revelation of Jesus Christ,**"* (Galatians 1:11-12).

In this prayer book, I am going to share a certain kind of prayer with you called Morning Time Prayer, or Fourth Watch Prayer, that Jesus taught me face to face. In a series of visitations, Jesus taught me about a special form and kind of prayer that is needed for the new move to be birthed right. He came to me in a dream in my late teens and started teaching me about morning prayer. Then He came back a few years later, explaining to me the magnitude of morning prayer. In Chapter 1, I will share these two visitations, and expound further on the revelations that I got from those visitations in the remaining chapters.

CHAPTER 1
The Wings of the Morning

CHAPTER 1
The Wings of the Morning

Jesus Appears to Me About Morning Prayer

I was doing shut-in prayer on and off in a church up north in Port Huron, Michigan from 2005 until 2007 when the Lord visited me in a dream. At times, I was staying for a night, three days, seven days, and other times I stayed for two weeks. The apostle in charge of that church allowed me to come in and stay in the basement of the church and shut-in to pray. I started this long season of prayer in 2005 and it was now 2007. I was praying during this season because I had a lot of questions. I was seeking God to get confirmation about major prophecies and dreams He gave me from 2000 to 2003.

People that are connected to me were constantly having visitations from Jesus. He would take them to Heaven or visit them in dreams about my future. These visitations they were having were so powerful and out of this world, I struggled to believe them because I thought that maybe they were trying to encourage me or were receiving dreams out of their own spirit because they loved my ministry. I really wanted to confirm what the Lord was telling them about me. I like to confirm whatever God is saying because as Jesus said, *"... in the mouth of two or three witnesses every word may be established,"* (Matthew 18:16).

I was extremely interested in a trip to Heaven the Lord gave to a little boy who was the son of one of my staff members. Jesus took him to Heaven and gave him a message and revelation of the Latter Rain End-Time move to give to me. Jesus revealed to this little boy that the Latter Rain is not just an outpouring of the Holy Ghost, but an outpouring of Jehovah. The Latter Rain move is about Jehovah coming down to earth, face to face, with mankind. Jesus said to the little boy, *"Come with me, I want to show you the greatest End Time Move of God that is going to hit the earth and it is David's destiny to lead it."* Then the Lord allowed a portal to open, and they looked down and saw earth. People were emptying out of all the nations of the world and coming to St. Louis because the Father came down and was openly, physically working with me openly as He did with Moses!

During these shut-ins, I asked God how He was going to come down and work with me, because I had no beginning point of reference to even begin to believe God to do it, and Jesus came and explained to me how it would happen. He told me I must develop meekness before God would come down visibly and notably to work with me before multitudes. In 2006, the Father came down for the first time with me in Spokane, Washington. In that appearance, the Father's face appeared as a rainbow of fire for a whole hour and jewels fell from the sky as He appeared. It was so notable and National Geographic featured a picture of this appearance. I wanted more! I wanted what God gave Moses and I kept seeking the Lord because I did not want just a onetime visitation, I wanted the Father to keep coming down with me on earth and appear everywhere I go.

Morning Time Prayer Accelerates You

In 2007, I spent even more time doing long seasons of prayer in the church in Port Huron. I was seeking God about my destiny, asking Him to give me a spiritual checkup because I sensed I was behind, but did not know where or how. I prayed, *"Lord I need to get up to speed. I need to get my destiny back on track. Please help me."* After that prayer, Jesus appeared to me in a dream and lifted me off the

The Wings of the Morning

ground, ascending me into the sky to meet Him. He was wearing a very beautiful and gorgeous white robe. As we stood face to face, He said to me, "David, you are about two years behind in your destiny."

Some people do not even know if they are behind or whether they are accurately following the will of God for their life or not. A lot of preachers are ministering outside of God's will. Preaching the gospel does not mean that you are in God's perfect will, you can be working for God and still not be in His will. You need to pray, *"Lord I want your will for my life."* David is a prime example of someone who aggressively pursued the will of God for his life. He said, *"Teach me to do thy will; for thou art my God..."* (Psalm 143:10). Because of this heart and prayer, David never lost a battle and why God loved him so much!

When Jesus said, *"You are two years behind in my will,"* I was so surprised. I asked, *"Lord, two years?"* He said, *"Yes you are two years behind in your destiny."* His face was shining as He spoke with me and He was not condemning me in any way. He was kind and loving and said, *"I did not just come to tell you that you are behind time, I have come to show you how to catch up."*

People have been delayed many years in their destiny and don't know it because they do not have visitations like this! <u>Prayer is what helps to keep you on course with your destiny.</u> <u>The revelations, instructions, and answers you get in prayer help you stay in God's will</u>. If you feel you've been delayed and hindered from staying on track with God's will for your life, keep reading because I am going to show you how to catch up the same way the Lord told me.

Jesus stood before me, regally and majestically, in this dream and said, *"David, I have come to give you the answer and wisdom on how to catch up. You must wake up at 3 a.m. every day and pray until the breaking of day. Whenever you wake up early in the morning and pray until daybreak, you are meeting Me at My time. The morning time is My time and that is when I choose to visit you. When you get up at any other time of the day or evening you are meeting Me on your time. At noon and in the evening is 'your' time to pray and visit me. David, you must get up very early. If you do this you will catch up."*

THE WINGS OF THE MORNING

Jesus said this to me as He stood in the sky with His face glowing majestically. I was overwhelmed He stood there as regal as ever, yet so humble, meek, loving, and gentle. He spoke like a king also like a friend.

The Lord pointed with His right index finger at the wing of a private jet passing by and said, *"Whenever you get up at 3 a.m. and pray until the breaking of day, it's like you're taking a jet to get to your destination."* He looked at me and asked, *"How much quicker is that?"* I responded, *"So you are telling me that when I get up in the morning to pray my speed will increase spiritually?"* He nodded and said, *"Yes, you may be behind but if you get on this jet you will go faster. Praying in the morning speeds you up."*

Then Jesus showed me a map of the United States and pointed first at St. Louis and then at Texas and said to me, *"When you get up to meet me in prayer early in the morning and don't miss this visitation it's like taking a private jet from St. Louis to Texas rather than taking a bus or a car to get there. You move at a faster pace and at a quicker speed to the location you need to get to because the morning speeds you up. But when you pray at other times of the day, it is like taking a bus or a car to your destination and it takes a long time."*

As the Lord was sharing all this with me He said, *"You can take the wings of the morning, or you can take a set of wheels which are slower."* The old folks used to say, *"We've got to keep the prayer wheels turning."* That is talking about praying at other times of the day. When you get up to pray from 3 a.m. until the break of day, you accelerate. You do not travel with wheels, you fly with the wings and you will make greater progress! The morning time visitation is a wing that accelerates you to your destiny!

Wings of the Morning in Scripture

When I woke up from that dream I said, *"Oh God, this is amazing!"* I got the point that Jesus was making about how the morning speeds you up, but I didn't know where the revelation was in scripture. One thing I have experienced with the Lord is that whenever He appears to you, He does not need to give you a scripture because He is the Word of God! However, you still need to find the scripture, not only for your edification and understanding, but for other people's as well. Dreams contain a lot of symbolism, and when they are from God, you will find them in scripture.

I asked the Holy Spirit to show me where this experience was in God's Word. I am a Word person and I do not put revelations I get in dreams over the Word of God. The Holy Spirit brought a scripture to me that I remembered reading a long time ago, **"If I take the wings of the morning..."** (Psalm 139:9)

I was so excited to find that scripture in the Bible. Rising up early in the morning and praying till daybreak is like taking the wings of the morning! I said, *"Oh what revelation! This is exactly what Jesus was saying! The morning time has wings!"* In other words, you travel at a faster pace in the spirit when you pray in the mornings.

When you pray in the morning, time flies by so quickly because of the glorious physical presence of the Lord on the earth at that time. If you do not get up early in the morning you miss God because the fourth watch is when He visits the earth.

The Strategical Speed of Fourth Watch Prayer

You must understand that you can be unaware that you are behind in your destiny, but this revelation about fourth watch prayer can catch you up. This is a major blessing of the morning time visitation, and when you start meeting God at the time He visits the earth, He will give you strategic wisdom and shortcuts to accelerate you and give you the ear and tongue of the learned to hear and understand things on a very high level so you will catch up. The Bible says, **"See then that ye walk circumspectly, not as fools, but as wise, Redeeming the time,** *because the days are evil. Wherefore be ye not unwise, but understanding what the will of the Lord is,"* (Ephesians 5:15-17).

Wisdom redeems time and helps you understand God's will for your life and what you need to do to recover lost time in your destiny.

God knows where to send you if you are behind. He knows what to tell you that will get you to the place in ministry where you need to be.

The strategical speed and acceleration of fourth watch prayer is to divinely accelerate and help you catch up if you have fallen behind in your destiny. I want you to understand that you too can catch up when you specifically meet God during fourth watch prayer from 3 a.m. to the breaking of day.

Morning Wings Give You Superiority in the Air

Another reason why Jesus gave me this revelation in midair, with the private jet flying past us, is that when you get up to pray at 3 a.m. until the breaking of day, you are operating in the heavenlies, far above every blockage that has been working against you on the ground! During fourth watch, God gives you superiority in the air against principalities and powers in heavenly places.

When Satan sees you doing this kind of prayer, He elevates his attacks and also gets in the air. Over the years, I've noticed that whenever I did fourth watch prayer, I started overcoming ground attacks, people saying evil things against me, but then right after that, I started going through media attacks. Satan, the prince of the power of the air, gets up in the air and fights me. However, he doesn't stop God's superiority in the air. Fourth watch is when God comes down on the earth to visit man. That is the time He goes forth as the Bible says *"... his going forth is prepared as the morning,"* (Hosea 6:3). Nothing can stop His superiority in the air. The Bible says, *"... the upright shall have dominion over them in the morning,"* (Psalm 49:14).

You must understand that the fourth watch is not about *your* superiority in the air, it is about God's and it causes the righteous to have dominion in the morning over whatever attack Satan brings in the air! When Satan elevates the attack, you get into fourth watch prayer God just takes you higher, faster. It's like when the devil starts using planes God starts using rockets. Satan can never trump God. The acceleration and superiority you have in the fourth watch is not limited to the wings of the morning or a jet. When the devil starts speeding up, you speed up at a greater pace because *"... where sin abounded, grace did much more abound!"* (Romans 5:20). No matter what the devil does to catch up to where you are, as long as you get up to pray from 3 a.m. until the breaking of day, God gives you something faster and does something greater to get you to where you are going! When I started doing what the Lord commanded me everything just started happening. If you want your business or ministry to grow at an astronomical rate, just get up in the morning, meet God, and pray till daybreak.

3 am Prayer Takes You Into the Future

Now, 3 am prayer can catch you up if you are behind, but it does so much more than that, it also propels you and takes care of your future. This kind of prayer can speed you up from where you are behind and speed you into the future if you are already caught up. This helps pave your way into the future. And this is where we have to change. There are way too many believers lagging in their destiny. It's time for us to stop operating in deficit and start operating in surplus, whereby we operate on being ahead. For example, the prophet Daniel prayed so much he was allowed to go beyond his generation and see four hundred and ninety years of Israel's future (Daniel 9:24-27). This is also known as the 70-week prophecy in which each week represents seven years making up 490 years. Daniel got so far out into the future he was told he had gone far enough because now he was intruding into the end of times.

> *"And I heard, but I understood not: then said I, O my Lord, what shall be the end of these things? And he said,* **Go thy way, Daniel: for the words are closed up and sealed till the time of the end,"** *(Daniel 12:8-9).*

You see this with Enoch also. He walked so close to God and got to the point where God began speaking to him about the end times. He went beyond Daniel because he paid the price in prayer for much longer than Daniel did. I believe Daniel as a public official and a Prime Minister in the Persian Empire could not spend as much time in prayer as Enoch did. Enoch walked so close with God he began to go beyond his generation far into the timeline of God's plan for the earth that God could trust him with revelations about the end times and the second coming of the Lord Jesus Christ. Enoch prophesied about how at the end of times the Lord will come with myriads of saints to execute judgment on earth, *"And Enoch also, the seventh from Adam, prophesied of these, saying, Behold, the Lord cometh with ten thousands of his saints, To execute judgment upon all ..."* (Jude 1:14-15).

This scripture is actually a quote from the ancient book of Enoch. The book of Enoch and the book of Jasher are extrabiblical accounts of Enoch's life details how Enoch spent years shut away in a house, away from all people, and alone with God. That is how he walked with God. Having spent years and years shut away with God he began to operate in "Time Surplus" as I call it. Shutting away for many years put him ahead to where his prayers did not only cover and bathe his whole life including the end of his life, but these prayers also went into the future and started giving him rewards where God basically said, *"Okay I can translate you. Your prayers have reached into eternity."* Enoch's future in the next life was affected by his prayers. He began to operate so far in the future God simply took him away. Those who spend long seasons of prayer with the Lord can be used to pave the way for future generations of believers.

Elijah was also known to shut himself away in the cave at Horeb to spend time with God, that is why he was also accounted worthy to be translated. You have to prepare to be translated like this. Since 2020 I have been shut away in a church for more than a year and a half and still counting and I have noticed that now I am having dreams of God already packing out all the arenas for the Arena Miracle Crusades coming up for years to come. I have been praying for the move of God that is about to hit America and the rest of the world and God promised me that all the arenas we rent out will be packed out.

You see, God can promise you things, but it does not have to happen. You must pay the price in prayer for God to do what he promised you. I have noticed that whenever I seek God in fourth watch prayer what He promises come to pass. That is why the devil fights to keep us out of spending time with God like this because prayer changes everything. Prayer either changes you or the circumstances you are dealing with. Either way, you will have victory when you enter this kind of prayer. There is no way you can lose when you dedicate yourself to fourth watch prayer!

Major Breakthroughs Happened When I Obeyed Jesus
The Birthing of the Face to Face Book

After that visitation, the Lord gave me wisdom to redeem time when I started doing fourth watch prayer. Amazing things suddenly began to happen and everything in my life changed! Everything I lost was restored and doors that were shut suddenly opened. Yes, I lost two years, but I got it back in no time!

The Lord visited me and instructed me to write the bestselling book, *Face to Face Appearances from Jesus: The Ultimate Intimacy* in September 2007 and said, *"Write the Face to Face book and be finished by December."* I had a three-month deadline to finish it. That is the acceleration that accompanies fourth watch prayer. When you start doing this, the Lord will visit you and give you strategical details concerning timing.

Everything was about timing and a supernatural grace came upon me to finish the book. I started writing on and off for several years and could not finish it, but after the Lord visited me, I was able to finish in three months! During that same time, Prophet Kim Clement prophesied about the great impact the book would have. He said *"God says, you carry on writing man. Because see, you have truth that must be written, and people must purchase, and they must read it. Even if you don't write it yourself. There is coming an opportunity that God is going to open for the truth and treasure that's inside of you to be put onto paper."* It was a great confirmation. I received that prophetic word because I was doing fourth watch prayer!

By December, I was finished writing the book as the Lord instructed, but I did not know what to do to get it published. I remembered the prophet said God would open an opportunity for me to get the book out. The pastor of the church hosting me for a series of services said to me, *"You need to get the book published."* But I didn't know what to do about that. He said, *"Well, why don't we go to Destiny Image. I will go up there with you."* The pastor went with me to Destiny Image and we gave them the book. Come to find out, the very day we got there it was the cutoff date for them to receive books that were to be published that year.

If I did not finish the book by December, I would have missed the cut off date! Jesus wanted me to finish the book by December because He wanted the book out the next year. Destiny Image accepted the book and in December 2009 they published it. The book went viral and it spread everywhere and became an instant bestseller. Do you see how quickly things opened for me after I started doing fourth watch prayer as the Lord instructed me? I caught up to my destiny in no time.

Once that book hit the market, I became known all over the world and my ministry blew up nationally and internationally! It was morning prayer that caused Jesus to visit me and give me strategy and wisdom about what book to write. I had a lot of books in me and I could have released any one of them, but it would never have gotten the success that the face to face book did. Writing the right book is what shot me forward and gave me success!

God Gave Me What Moses Had

Another amazing thing that happened was that the Lord visited me again to talk about Moses. During fourth watch I was praying about a powerful visitation I had in 2006, when I was shut in the church and Jesus walked through the wall and appeared to me while I doing a shutin at the church and said, *"A 400-year period just passed by. This is the 400th year of America's existence. David, 400 years passed by before the first appearance of the Lord in Spokane, Washington. There is a 400-year interval before the Father comes down just like it was in Moses' time and in my time. You are the prophet that God has chosen to lead this face to face movement. You are a face to face prophet. My Father and I, we are going to start coming down to work with you. We will start appearing openly in the clouds before all three hundred and seventy million Americans."*

This came as a revelation to me. I had no idea that I was a face to face prophet, and I did not even know what that meant. Jesus had to teach me about who a face to face prophet is because the fivefold ministry today does not teach on this. In this visitation, He led me to Deuteronomy 34:10 which states, **"And there arose not a prophet since in Israel like unto Moses, whom the LORD knew face to face."** A face to face prophet is someone who has a special ministry of being face to face with

God like Moses was and who has the power to bring others face to face with God. After this visitation, someone told me about a prophecy given by a major prophet. This person prophesied that God revealed to him that in the last days the Lord will raise up a ministry like that of Moses and that a black man will be leading that movement.

This is what I was praying about and seeking God to do in my life. In 2007, when I started doing fourth watch prayer, I asked the Lord to give me what Moses had like He promised to do in 2006. It is important to never assume that because you have a visitation or a prophecy about something you automatically have the manifestation. God made several amazing promises to Israel about His plan to restore them to the land of Canaan after they were in exile for 70 years, but He also said, *"... I will yet for this be enquired of by the house of Israel, to do it for them; I will increase them with men like a flock,"* (Ezekiel 36:37). You must seek God for what He promised to do in your life! When I started getting up at 3 a.m. to pray until daybreak, the Lord came to me a few weeks later and said, *"I have now given you what Moses had."*

This happened a few weeks after the Lord visited me and told me that I was two years behind and to write the face to face book in three months. Jesus promised me that He would visit every person who reads the book. Immediately, He started visiting people in dreams and in the physical realm after they read the book. Some only read a few pages! Just as Moses brought God face to face with the people of his generation, I am bringing my generation face to face with the Lord both physically and in dreams. The Father began appearing in thick clouds, showing He's working openly with me. These manifestations intensified after I did morning time visitation prayer. The Face to Face Movement is about arranging a meeting between God and man!

How It All Began
Jesus Talks to Me About Morning Prayer in 1997

The first visitation I had about morning prayer was in 1997. I went to sleep and was immediately in a night vision. Jesus was wearing the most beautiful white robe I have ever seen. He was sitting on a big rock with His head in His hand, looking in the opposite direction from where I was. I was puzzled and didn't understand why He was not looking at me. I was disturbed because the essence of the face to face relationship is His face. When the Lord knows you face to face, His face is turned to you. *"And the LORD spake unto Moses face to face, as a man speaketh unto his friend,"* (Exodus 33:11). He was looking the opposite way and I knew something was wrong.

Before this visitation, I slacked up in my morning prayer time. Since the Lord saved me, I prayed 3 times a day in the morning, afternoon, and then late at night before I went to sleep. I was moved to do this when I read about how David prayed three times a day.

"Evening, and morning, and at noon, will I pray, and cry aloud: and he shall hear my voice" (Psalm 55:17). Daniel also had this devotional lifestyle. Daniel *"kneeled upon his knees three times a day, and prayed..."* (Daniel 6:10). I vowed to pray every day from 17 to 24 years of age, I constantly prayed and never missed my times with the Lord.

My prayer life increased as the Lord started appearing to me regularly. The more He appeared to me the more I pursued Him. I spent hundreds of hours in my room fellowshipping with Jesus and would not come out. It was so tremendous and amazing things were happening to me. My room filled with mist and smoke from the glory of God as I met with Him in prayer. When my friends would visit, they could not get in because the glory was so strong. They would fall on the floor! They didn't know what was knocking them down, and at the time, I didn't know either. I was from the Baptist church we didn't know anything about being slain in the spirit. You have to be built for glory. The more time you spend in God's presence, the more you can withstand and carry the glory.

In Heaven, certain angels cannot stand directly in the presence of God, and other angels are built in a special way to withstand more glory, and there are even greater angels who are called face to face angels. They stand before God and behold His face continually (Matthew 18:10). I was spending so much time with God I lost track of time. For seven to eight years, I spent more than ten hours a day, at times fourteen, and even eighteen hours a day fellowshipping with the

The Wings of the Morning

Lord. At points, my parents were really concerned about me and thought I was not spending enough time with people. Maybe I was a little bit unbalanced then, but I know every second I spent in the Lord's presence was worth it! And to this very day, even with a global ministry, I still take time to go and spend time with the Lord and shut away in a church for weeks and months at a time.

After about eight years of constant prayer, I slacked up for two weeks and unknowingly grieved the Lord! I was still praying long hours, but I stopped praying in the mornings like I used to. At that time, I didn't have the revelation of morning time visitation prayer like I do now. I thought I could reach God at any time, and yes, we can go boldly before God at any time, but there are certain times that have greater weight with Him. It was slacking off in the mornings and some evenings for those two weeks that the Lord came to me in the dream and was grieved. He did not say anything to me, and after an awkward moment of silence, I said to Jesus, *"Lord, I miss you."* Without turning to look at me, He answered, *"Yes, I miss you too, and the times we used to spend in the mornings."*

When you slack up in your prayer life with the Lord you begin to feel it. Carnal believers who do not pray like this will have no idea what I am talking about, but when you have a consistent prayer life with God and slack up for a day or two, especially a week, you start missing His presence. During those two weeks, I stopped praying in the mornings, but I was still praying most afternoons and evenings and I thought it was okay until the Lord visited me and said He missed the times we spent in the mornings!

My heart dropped and I woke out of that dream crying. I looked at the time and it was 3 a.m.! I jumped out of bed and rushed to my bathroom and got on my knees to pray. I also missed some of the noon and evening prayer times during that period, but Jesus never mentioned those times. He only mentioned the morning time. I was too young and immature at that time to fully understand the revelation. The visitation did not last a long time, but it changed my life and shook me.

THE WINGS OF THE MORNING

Jesus is a Morning Person

Even though I never missed morning times like that again, I still did not understand the depth of what Jesus was saying to me. I thought He was saying I was slacking up on my morning prayer times and I simply needed to go back to praying in the morning. However, it was years later when I discovered the real reason why Jesus wanted me to pray in the morning. Morning time prayer is very important to Jesus because He is a morning person. Some people are not morning people, and I wasn't a morning person before the Lord started talking to me about rising up early to pray as He did during His earthly ministry.

> **"And in the morning, rising up a great while before day,** *he went out, and departed into a solitary place, and there prayed,"* (Mark 1:35).

Jesus got up at 3 in the morning, a great while before daybreak, and He would pray until sunrise because He knew the significance of morning prayer. This was Jesus' pattern when He was on the earth, and He is our greatest example. This "morning" prayer is not waking up to pray at 8 or 10 a.m. when the sun is already up. The scripture says, *"rising up a great while before day."* That means it was still dark outside and the sun was not up when Jesus got up to pray and it's known as Fourth Watch prayer in the Bible!

> *"And it came to pass in those days, that he went out into a mountain to pray,* ***and continued all night in prayer to God. And when it was day,*** *he called unto him his disciples: and of them he chose twelve, whom also he named apostles,"* (Luke 6:12-13).

In this scripture, you see that Jesus prayed all night until daybreak. There are seasons of prayer when God will have you wake up and continue all night in prayer. That is morning prayer!

Becoming a Vessel of Honor Through Morning Prayer

I had to change because I was used to staying up late and sleeping in until noon, like a lot of preachers do, because I didn't understand how important morning time prayer was until God corrected me with these powerful words, *"David, your ministry will never* be a ministry of honor if you do not get up in the morning." Those words pierced through my heart like a sword. I knew the scripture the Lord was referring to and immediately started studying to get more understanding.

> *"But in a great house there are not only **vessels of gold and of silver, but also of wood and of earth; and some to honour, and some to dishonour.** If a man therefore purge himself from these, he shall be **a vessel unto honour**, sanctified, and meet for the master's use, and prepared unto every good work,"*
> (2 Timothy 2:20-21).

One thing you must understand about the Lord's visitations is that Jesus is the Word of God and whenever He appears, you will find what He says in scripture. The scripture talks about the vessel of honor being purged and sanctified. I thought a vessel of honor referred to someone living right and holy until I looked up the meaning in the Greek. A vessel unto honor is a vessel fit for the master's use. The word honor "time" means a value, a price or money paid, valuable, esteem, dignity, honor precious. A vessel of honor is a ministry of great reputation that is highly valued and esteemed in the Body of Christ for the "master's use."

A master's degree is worth much more than a GED because it takes more time, years, and money to earn. When you are fit for the master's use, it is like having your master's degree or Ph.D. in the Holy Ghost. When you become a vessel of honor, God says, *"Now you are ready to be used for certain jobs that other people cannot do in my Kingdom."* On the other hand, a vessel of dishonor in the Greek is a vessel of low means or low rank. The word dishonor or "atimia" in the Greek means infamy, indignity, disgrace, shame, vile, or despised. In other words, when you are a vessel of dishonor, God keeps your ministry at a low rank and level.

Many leaders and pastors wonder why their ministry only gets to a certain level and they stay there for many years, limiting the ways God can use them. Then they comfort themselves by saying, *"I guess God called me to shepherd just 25 people, so I'm just going to be faithful here. Bless God, He has not called all of us to have huge ministries."* That is not

THE WINGS OF THE MORNING

true, the devil is lying to you. There is a stage in your spiritual development where the Lord expects you to be faithful when you are small and unknown. However, it is you that determines what level your ministry operates at, by whether you are willing to pay the price to be a vessel of honor or not. Do you want to have a ministry of honor? Do you want to get your master's degree or Ph.D. in the Spirit? Then study to show yourself approved unto God! When you get up and pray from 3 a.m. until dawn, and gain weight and substance in the spirit, you will have a ministry of honor to be used for His honorable purpose!

Bringing Balance to Daily Fourth Watch Prayer

*"And it came to pass **in those days,** that he went out into a mountain to pray, and continued all night in prayer to God. And when it was day, he called unto him his disciples..."* (Luke 6:12-13). There are seasons when God wants you to continue all night in prayer until daybreak, but He does not expect you to do this kind of prayer all the time, every day of your life. That is why the scripture says Jesus did this kind of prayer, ***"in those days."*** Rising early in the morning is a real challenge, if it wasn't a sacrifice, it wouldn't be worth anything. The high value of this kind of prayer is seen in *what* the Lord brings during His daily visitations to the earth. Jesus paid the price in His ministry through seasons of rising early to pray all night until the breaking of day, and a greater realm of anointing manifested as the crowds of sick people were healed, simply by touching Him (Luke 6:17-19). When you rise early in the morning you receive things you otherwise would not have. The sacrifice pays off!

God only requires you to do this kind of prayer in certain seasons or it will wear you out. He will give you time to rest and during those times, He will still meet you in your dreams (Job 7:17-18). When we are asleep, He does not neglect His morning visitation with us through dreams, and sometimes He does not show us anything He simply lets us rest.

Sometimes we miss our visitations from the Lord because we expect Him to come the same way, every day, every time. If you are sensitive to the Spirit, you will notice there are times when the Lord is saying, *"Get up now! You need to get up and meet me."* You will have a strong burden on you to pray and meet Him during the fourth watch. In fact, there will be times when God sends angelic messengers to wake you up as Zechariah the prophet experienced. *"And the angel that talked with me came again, and waked me, as a man that is wakened out of his sleep,"* (Zechariah 4:1).

There are other times and seasons that the Lord will lift off and let you rest. You will not be in prayer speaking words to Him, you will be in a season where you are receiving from Him. It is like exhaling and inhaling. When you exhale you are talking to God in prayer, but when you inhale, you are receiving and hearing from God. When the Lord wants you to rest from fourth watch prayer, you are receiving from Him. Rest is also a visitation from God. ***"... for so he giveth his beloved sleep,"*** (Psalm 127:2). God gives you rest because it is one of the ten commandments.

"Remember the sabbath day, to keep it holy. ***Six days shalt thou labour,*** *and do all thy work: But* ***the seventh day is the sabbath of the LORD thy God: in it thou shalt not do any work,*** *thou, nor thy son, nor thy daughter, thy manservant, nor thy maidservant, nor thy cattle, nor thy stranger that is within thy gates: For in six days the LORD made heaven and earth, the sea, and all that in them is,* ***and rested the seventh day:*** *wherefore the LORD blessed the sabbath day, and hallowed it,"* (Exodus 20:8-11).

The word Sabbath is the Hebrew word "shabbath" which really means "Intermission, to repose, cease or desist from exertion." The Sabbath is God giving you an intermission, a break, a pause from working. If God rested on the seventh day, after working for six days, He also desires to give you rest, but don't become slothful and lazy and say, *"Oh well, I can slack off from time to time and rest."* God commanded that the children of Israel work six days and rest one day. You must labor in the fourth watch prayer until God gives you leave to enter His rest for a time.

God Gives His Beloved Sleep

When the Lord first told me to do morning prayer I said, *"Lord do you mean we need to do this every morning? We need to rise up and meet you every morning at 3 a.m.?"* He said, *"David, that is not what I'm saying to you."* At this point, He gave me balance and understanding of this teaching. **"It is vain for you to rise up early, to sit up late, to eat the bread of sorrows: for so he giveth his beloved sleep,"** (Psalm 127:2). It is vain to go beyond what God desires you to do with this kind of prayer. Jesus did not even pray like this every day, He did it for a season (Luke 6:12-13). When the Spirit took me to that scripture I looked up and said, *"Lord do you mean that you didn't get up every night?"* Jesus answered, *"No, I didn't. I did the fourth watch prayer at certain seasons when the Father was pulling me into that fellowship."*

I know we have some carnal believers, that I call "flesh creatures," who are breathing a big sigh of relief and saying, *"Phewwww! We can relax and sleep. God wants us to sleep!"* God does want us to get up at 3 a.m. and pray until daybreak for long seasons of time, then there is a season when the grace is not on you, and He allows you to rest. Over the last 30 years, I have experienced times when I was so tired, and I knew God wanted me to get up to pray, but I didn't. When I woke up later that day, I would say to myself, *"Well, I will just mark that as a visitation of the rest."* However, it is not up to you or I to determine when we are in a visitation of rest, it is imperative to stay in God's timing and be synchronized with His leading. You cannot follow your body or flesh you must be led by the Spirit in doing early morning prayer.

Jesus is a Morning Person Like His Father

To understand the Lord; you must stop thinking of Him as an impersonal being, devoid of emotion or personality. He is a person and the reason why you experience hurt and have feelings is because you were made in His image and His likeness. Oftentimes, we separate ourselves from who He is, but we are made like God in so many ways.

Almost everything you see on earth with humans is displayed in heaven with God.

I have always loved waterfalls. The first house that was built for me had huge windows in the back that went up two stories and there was a huge lake in the backyard. I loved getting up in the morning to meditate while looking at the lake through the glass windows. I love water and anything I build has a water fountain or a lake of water around it. I thought that was just a personal preference of mine, until one morning when the Lord spoke to me while I was praying. He said, *"David, do you think you like looking over water just because you do? You only like looking over water because I like looking over water."* I asked, *"Lord, how?"* Then He brought up a revelation to me. He said, *"There is a sea of glass right before my throne!"* That really amazed me. The Father likes looking over water as He sits on His throne!

"And before the throne there was a sea of glass like unto crystal: *and in the midst of the throne, and round about the throne, were four beasts full of eyes before and behind,"* (Revelation 4:6).

Do you see how impersonal we have made God? You like things on Earth simply because He does. When you realize this, you will see it is part of God's image and likeness manifested in you.

After walking with God for more than 30 years, I have learned that He is a morning person. He sets out from His chambers early in the morning to visit man. **"... his going forth is prepared as the morning,"** (Hosea 6:3). It's part of God's daily routine! Another way to look at it, is to understand that Jesus is the express image of His Father. *"Who being the brightness of his glory,* **and the express image of his person..."** (Hebrews 1:3). Do you see how this scripture mentions the word "person?" The Lord is not just a deity, He is not an android sitting on a throne like religion has portrayed Him. He is a person and when you develop a face to face relationship with the Lord you get to know Him as such.

As the express image of the Father, Jesus mirrors what the Father does. During His earthly ministry, Jesus woke up while it was still dark outside and prayed until daybreak. He did this because as a true Son, Jesus does what the Father does. *"...Verily, verily, I say unto you, The Son can do nothing of himself, but what he seeth the Father do:* **for what things soever he doeth, these also doeth the Son likewise,"** (John 5:19). In other words, Jesus is saying, *"What you see Me do, I do because I saw my Father doing it."* The Father, Jesus, and the Holy Spirit are morning people!

THE WINGS OF THE MORNING

God the Father and Jesus <u>make special</u> trips from Heaven to the earth every morning, (causing a portal to open) that releases many different things to happen when they come on earth and I will expound upon them in the pages of this book. The morning time is God's appointment to meet with man and bless him with things that are not available at any other time of the day. He will give you strategic short cuts for your destiny and cause you to recover all that has been lost in your life!

CHAPTER 2
The Importance of the Watch and God's Visit

CHAPTER 2
The Importance of the Watch and God's Visit

"Therefore let us not sleep, as do others; but let us watch and be sober," (1 Thessalonians 5:6).

Jesus Commands Us to Watch and Pray

I need you to understand how important it is to watch! Jesus said, **"Watch ye therefore, and pray..."** (Luke 21:36). Jesus commands us not to just pray, but to watch. In fact, He mentions "watch" first! That means you need to watch to be able to pray! *"... watch unto prayer,"* (1 Peter 4:7). Watching is a command from Jesus for our spiritual walk with God. We must be alert and watch out for His return, known as the Rapture. *"Watch therefore, for ye know neither the day nor the hour wherein the Son of man cometh,"* (Matthew 25:13). Prayer must be coupled with watching to avoid temptations and not to miss the Lord's visitations.

*"**Watch and pray,** that ye enter not into temptation: the spirit indeed is willing, but the flesh is weak,"* (Matthew 26:41).

*"**Take ye heed, watch and pray:** for ye know not when the time is,"* (Mark 13:33).

*"**Watch ye and pray,** lest ye enter into temptation. The spirit truly is ready, but the flesh is weak,"* (Mark 14:38).

This is not just for apostles, men and women of God, "prayer warriors," or serious believers, it is for all believers! Jesus commanded the twelve apostles to watch and pray. *"And what I say unto you I say unto all, Watch,"* (Mark 13:37). His command is to you as well! Watching is often mentioned parallel and synonymous with prayer in the Bible. If Jesus says to watch and pray, it means you cannot pray effectively without watching, and you need to watch in order to pray!

The word "watch' in Greek is *gregoreuō* and it means "to keep awake, to be vigilant, and to be watchful." It also means to rouse from sleep, to give strict attention to, to be cautious, active (Strong's Concordance). To watch also means "to take heed lest through remission and indolence some destructive calamity suddenly overtake one." (Thayer's Greek Definitions G1127). Below is a list of what the word "watch" means, and you need to get understanding of them all:

- To be sleepless or to be awake and watching (Matthew 26:38, 40-41)
- To be circumspect, which means to be attentive and ready with faith (1 Corinthians 16:13)
- To exercise constant vigilance over something (Hebrews 13:17)
- Wariness: To be cautious about possible dangers or problems. It's the characteristic of being very careful or cautious against spiritual dangers and beguilements from the devil (1 Peter 5:8; Mark 13:33-37)
- To take heed and watch (Mark 13:33-37)
- To stay awake and pray. To watch or to be vigilant in prayer. (Matthew 26:41; 1 Peter 5:8)

To watch means to stay awake. *"... except the LORD keep the city, the watchman waketh but in vain,"* (Psalm 127:1). When you watch and pray as Jesus told His disciples, you experience major blessings. *"Watch ye therefore, and pray always, that ye may be accounted worthy to escape all these things that shall come to pass, and to stand before the Son of man,"* (Luke 21:36).

The Importance of the Watch and God's Visit

Jesus uses the word "always" when He is revealing a lifestyle you must establish to avoid certain things that can happen to you and to come into major things you need in your life. Jesus mentions three things that watching causes in your life:

- Causes you to be accounted worthy
- Causes you to escape
- Causes you to stand before the Lord

These blessings are powerful, and every Christian needs them in their life. When you watch you gain value and weight in the spirit and your ministry becomes a proven through honor. Watching also causes you to escape danger, disaster, and temptation, enables you to see clearly in the spirit, and your discernment is sharpened. Watching also causes you to stand before the Lord either through visions, trips to Heaven, or face to face!

Watch and Pray to Avoid Temptation

"Watch and pray, that ye enter not into temptation: the spirit indeed is willing, but the flesh is weak," (Matthew 26:41).

Jesus deems watching to be so important in avoiding temptation, that He went back to wake up His disciples three times in the garden of Gethsemane and was disappointed when He found them sleeping. The Bible says, *"And he cometh unto the disciples, and findeth them asleep, and saith unto Peter, **What, could ye not watch with me one hour?**"* (Matthew 26:40). Because they did not wake up to watch with Him, they all fell into temptation.

*"Behold, I come as a thief. **Blessed is he that watcheth, and keepeth his garments**, lest he walk naked, and they see his shame,"* (Revelation 16:15).

Jesus was revealing that watching is the payment for keeping your garments and it also avoids spiritual nakedness, shame, and disgrace. When you do not watch the thief comes and you lose a lot in life. You become impoverished and are no longer vigilant in the spirit. ***"His watchmen are blind: they are all ignorant, they are all dumb dogs, they cannot bark; sleeping, lying down, loving to slumber,"*** (Isaiah 56:10). Jesus wanted the disciples to watch and pray because He did not want them to become dumb blind dogs! When you do not watch you become lukewarm in the spirit and *"... wretched, and miserable, and poor, and blind, and naked,"* (Revelation 3:17).

If you get up to pray and sleep, you are not watching and praying, you are sleeping on the job. Keeping watch is a military precautionary measure to prevent surprise attacks. In the Bible, watchers were stationed to look out for the enemy. When the army was out for war and made camp at night, they broke the night into four watches of three hours each. During each watch, a company of warriors or soldiers stand guard, looking out for the enemy, until the next watch replaces them, which is known as the changing of the guard and is usually the time the enemy strikes. For example, when Gideon attacked the Midianites. *"... they had but newly set the watch,"* (Judges 7:19). During the days of Nehemiah, they set watches around the clock.

*"Nevertheless we made our prayer unto our God, **and set a watch against them day and night, because of them,"*** (Nehemiah 4:9).

Nehemiah instituted a watch, day and night to look out for the enemy, because the nations surrounding Israel wanted to destroy them. Watches were equally critical and important for the survival of a city and an army, just as watching is of highest importance to a believer. Throughout the New Testament, the believer is instructed and commanded to watch. Terms like "be sober," "be vigilant," and "keep the lamps burning," are used when giving instructions about watching because if you sleep, when you should be watching, you lose a lot. When you watch, you gain victory and blessings.

Benefits and Blessings of Watching

- **You receive your visitation:** *"Watch therefore, for ye know neither the day nor the hour wherein the Son of man cometh,"* (Matthew 25:13).

- **The Lord will personally minister to you:** *"Blessed are those servants, whom the lord when he cometh shall find watching: verily I say unto you, that he shall gird*

- **You escape the great tribulation:** *"Watch ye therefore, and pray always, that ye may be accounted worthy to escape all these things that shall come to pass, and to stand before the Son of man,"* (Luke 21:36).

- **You get blessed:** *"And if he shall come in the second watch, or come in the third watch, and find them so, blessed are those servants,"* (Luke 12:38).

- **Many days and years are covered in a night watch:** *"For a thousand years in thy sight are but as yesterday when it is past, and as a watch in the night,"* (Psalm 90:4).

- **You find life and obtain God's favor:** *"Blessed is the man that heareth me, watching daily at my gates, waiting at the posts of my doors. For whoso findeth me findeth life, and shall obtain favour of the LORD,"* (Proverbs 8:34-35).

- **Your ministry becomes proven:** *"But in all things approving ourselves as the ministers of God… in labours, in watchings, in fastings;"* (2 Corinthians 6:4-5). (2 Timothy 4:5)

- **You strengthen things that are about to die:** *"Be watchful, and strengthen the things which remain, that are ready to die…"* (Revelation 3:2).

Consequences of Not Watching

- **You miss your time of visitation:** *"Watch therefore: for ye know not what hour your Lord doth come,"* (Matthew 24:42).

- **You fall into temptation:** *"Watch and pray, that ye enter not into temptation…"* (Matthew 26:41).

- **You become naked, suffering shame and exposure:** *"Behold, I come as a thief. Blessed is he that watcheth, and* *keepeth his garments, lest he walk naked, and they see his shame,"* (Revelation 16:15).

- **You get snared in the troubles of the End Times:** *"And take heed to yourselves, lest at any time your hearts be overcharged with surfeiting, and drunkenness, and cares of this life, and so that day come upon you unawares. For as a snare shall it come on all them that dwell on the face of the whole earth,"* (Luke 21:34-35).

- **Your house gets broken into:** *"And this know, that if the goodman of the house had known what hour the thief would come, he would have watched, and not have suffered his house to be broken through,"* (Luke 12:39).

- **You become poor:** *"Yet a little sleep, a little slumber, a little folding of the hands to sleep: So shall thy poverty come as one that travelleth, and thy want as an armed man,"* (Proverbs 6:10-11). *"... and drowsiness shall clothe a man with rags,"* (Proverbs 23:21).

- **God will require the loss of life at your hand:** *"But if the watchman see the sword come, and blow not the trumpet, and the people be not warned; if the sword come, and take any person from among them, he is taken away in his iniquity;* ***but his blood will I require at the watchman's hand,****"* (Ezekiel 33:6).

Watching in Ministry

*"**Take ye heed, watch and pray: for ye know not when the time is.** For the Son of man is as a man taking a far journey, who left his house, and gave authority to his servants, and to every man his work, **and commanded the porter to watch. Watch ye therefore:** for ye know not when the master of the house cometh, at even, or at midnight, or at the cockcrowing, or in the morning: Lest coming suddenly he find you sleeping. **And what I say unto you I say unto all, Watch,**"* (Mark 13:33-37).

Watching in prayer is a critical part of a believer's life as well as a vital necessity in a minister's life. Jesus commanded His apostles to watch and pray many times. This command to watch was not just for the first 12 apostles, it is for all apostles and fivefold ministry officers, as payment to manifest the power of the office they walk in.

*"But in all things approving ourselves as the ministers of God, in much patience, in afflictions, in necessities, in distresses, In stripes, in imprisonments, in tumults, in labours, **in watchings**, in fastings,"* (2 Corinthians 6:4-5).

Ministers are proven and approved for ministry "in watchings." Notice watchings has an "s," meaning a minister needs to watch in prayer often. Paul pairs watchings and fastings because they are both part of prayer and he talks about the labors of a minister, "watchings" being one of them.

*"In weariness and painfulness, **in watchings often**, in hunger and thirst, in fastings often, in cold and nakedness,"* (2 Corinthians 11:27).

As a minister, if you do not watch, you will suffer loss in ministry. Jesus spoke about this when He spoke about porters who are given authority by a master to keep a house. Those porters are ministers and servants that Jesus leaves in charge of the people of God and it applies to parents who are heads of households. *"But know this, that if the goodman of the house had known in what watch the thief would come, **he would have watched, and would not have suffered his house to be broken up**,"* (Matthew 24:43). If church and ministry leaders do not watch and pray, then the church, ministry, or movement they oversee will be attacked and there will be much loss.

The Night Watches

*"When I remember thee upon my bed, and meditate on thee in **the night watches**."* (Psalm 63:6).

During the night there are four watches and David talks about staying awake to meditate on the Lord during the night watches. *"**Mine eyes prevent the night watches, that I might meditate in thy word**,"* (Psalm 119:148). Watching is not only connected to prayer, it is connected to meditation. It is remembering the Lord, thinking upon Him and what He's done in your life, and constructing a memorial of Him in your life.

THE WINGS OF THE MORNING

You should watch to wait on the Lord in meditation during the night hours but watching in most cases is complimentary to prayer.

*"Watch ye therefore: for ye know not when the master of the house cometh, at **even**, or at **midnight**, or at the **cockcrowing**, or in the **morning**,"* (Mark 13:35).

1. The Evening Watch (6 p.m. to 9 p.m.)
2. The Midnight Watch (9 p.m. to 12 a.m.)
3. The Cockcrowing (12 a.m. to 3 a.m.)
4. The Fourth or Morning Watch (3 a.m. to 6 a.m.)

There are blessings connected to each of these watches and special blessings for praying through all these watches at one time, known as All Night Prayer, that continues until daybreak. David kept all the night watches just so he could meditate on the Lord (Psalm 119:148). Jesus also spending all night in prayer.

*"And it came to pass in those days, that he went out into a mountain to pray, **and continued all night in prayer to God,**"* (Luke 6:12).

When Jesus did all night prayer for several days in a row, He entered another dimension of ministry. In my earlier days, I was experiencing low attendance in my crusades and Jesus came and told me that if I did what He did, praying all night until daybreak, the crowds would return. I continued all night watching and praying. That is why Jesus commands us to watch and pray. You watch to pray, if you do not watch or stay awake, you cannot pray.

If you want to break into certain levels, dimensions, and realms of ministry, and overcome insurmountable odds, you must practice the watch. Each watch of the night has its own blessings. The midnight watch gives you the awesome blessings of importunity. Jesus spoke of a friend who received a visitor and needed help to take care of him. The man went to his friend at midnight and asked him for three loaves of bread. Eventually, his friend gave him all that he needed.

The Importance of the Watch and God's Visit

*"I say unto you, Though he will not rise and give him, because he is his friend, **yet because of his importunity** he will rise and give him as many as he needeth,"* (Luke 11:8).

Midnight prayer is great when you have an emergency and need immediate help. God hears your prayer not just because you are a friend but because of your importunity. Why importunity? Because the rewards of praying during the midnight watch are awesome! The man received *"as many as he needeth."* During Passover, God executed judgment on the gods of Egypt and killed the firstborn at midnight. Jesus told His disciples that if He comes to find them keeping the night watches, specifically the second and third watches, He would personally minister to their needs!

*"Blessed are those servants, whom the lord when he cometh shall find watching: verily I say unto you, that he shall gird himself, and make them to sit down to meat, and will come forth and serve them. **And if he shall come in the second watch, or come in the third watch,** and find them so, blessed are those servants,"* (Luke 12:37-38).

How would you like for the Lord to come and personally minister to you and serve you with what you need? That is a specific blessing of the night watches. You can and should expect all the blessings and rewards that come with each watch to manifest in your life when you keep the night watches. However, the most important watch of the night is the last watch, being the Fourth Watch

The Fourth Watch

*"And he saw them toiling in rowing; for the wind was contrary unto them: **and about the fourth watch of the night** he cometh unto them, walking upon the sea, and would have passed by them,"* (Mark 6:48).

The fourth watch is specifically from 3 a.m. to 6 a.m. or daybreak and is the most powerful watch of the night, because it is when God comes down from heaven to physically visit man on earth. Not just His presence, but His person. Therefore, the greatest breakthroughs, miracles, and works of God are performed because you rise and meet God when He is on the earth! I call it Early Morning Visitation Prayer because you are meeting with God. It is supernatural and you get more done in the Spirit at that time than at any other time of the day or night.

The Lord came to one of my staff members in a dream and said, *"One 3 a.m. watch equals 12 days."* When the Lord said that to her she knew that was the timeframe for catching up what she was behind in. I know that was a specific word to her based on the stage of her spiritual growth because when you become fully spiritually mature just one watch in the night will equate to a thousand years in the spirit! *"For a thousand years in thy sight are ... as a watch in the night"* (Psalm 90:4). If keeping any one of the night watches covers a thousand years, then what about the Fourth Watch when Jehovah is physically on earth?

God's Daily Schedule

Don't ever think that God does not have a schedule for things on earth. He has a schedule that He keeps to because He is a God of order not confusion. *"For God is not the author of confusion ..."* (1 Corinthians 14:33). God is a good steward of every day because times and seasons belong to Him and He has rules that govern every detail of each day.

"... let not the sun go down upon your wrath," (Ephesians 4:26). You have until sundown to forgive everybody of anything they have done to you in a day. If you don't, you have just entered another day with anger. **"And the evening and the morning were the first day,"** (Genesis 1:5). And Jesus speaking about the day said, *"... Are there not twelve hours in the day?"* (John 11:9). You must understand that the way God calculates days is different than the way we do.

We think the day begins at dawn, but God's day ends at dawn! This is because God's Kingdom is different from the way things are done on earth.

"Let the wicked forsake his way, and the unrighteous man his thoughts: and let him return unto the LORD, and he will have mercy upon him; and to our God, for he will abundantly pardon. **For my thoughts are not your thoughts, neither are your ways my ways, saith the LORD.** *For as the heavens are higher than the earth, so are my ways higher than your ways, and my thoughts than your thoughts,"* (Isaiah 55:7-9).

Rising a great while before day, when most people are asleep, is part of us forsaking our ways and returning to the Lord. One of His ways that is different from ours is that He comes on the earth when sleep is sweetest, from 3 a.m. to 6 a.m. and expects man to rise at that time and meet up with Him. Doing so means that one is operating on God's schedule and adhering to His ways. Paul understood this. *"Therefore let us not sleep, as do others; but let us watch and be sober"* (1 Thessalonians 5:6). The word "watch" in the Greek is *gregoreuo* which means "to keep awake."

God gives rules governing the day. I want to help you understand why God puts such a premium on the early morning time of prayer. The Bible says God came into the garden in the cool of the day, we have understood that to be evening time, but if you understand what I just shared, you will understand that the cool of the day is at daybreak. This is always the coldest time of the night too!

God Visits Man Every Morning
There is a Special Time of Visitation in the Morning

When God created Adam, He established the routine of visiting man in the morning. I want you to imagine God Almighty and Jesus coming down from heaven together every single morning and around that time a portal from heaven is open as they walk in the cool of the day with Adam. He has not changed, He still does every morning, and He will faithfully keep His morning visitation schedule.

God makes this special trip from heaven to the earth just to see you. The angels in heaven wonder at this and ask why God has His

THE WINGS OF THE MORNING

heart set on man and visits Him every morning (Job 7:17-18). Even though Adam sinned and fell, God has not changed His mind. He devised a plan of salvation for us even during that time and does not come down here just to talk to animals, He comes to visit us. Will you be asleep when He comes in the morning and miss His visitation and dispensation?

Morning prayer is God's visit to the earth and Jesus knew it, that is why He got up to meet His Father a great while before daybreak. Don't misunderstand me, anytime you go to God in prayer He hears you, whether it is the morning, noon, evening, or midnight and He is known to answer His people at any time of the day. Elijah prayed during the evening sacrifice and God answered him with fire from heaven. What I am teaching is that praying from 3 a.m. to daybreak is the most effective time to pray because God is physically on the earth.

*"What is man, that thou shouldest magnify him? and that thou shouldest set thine heart upon him? And that **thou shouldest visit him every morning**, and try him every moment?"* (Job 7:17-18).

This key revelation is thrilling and most tremendous! Do you know that God has set His heart upon you? *"... and that thou shouldest set thine heart upon him."* God loves you so much that He travels from heaven to earth every morning to visit with you. How special and beautiful is that? It is super special, and therefore you should value the morning prayer visitation. Knowing this is the reason that I am often up at 3 a.m. to meet Him.

"And that thou shouldest visit him every morning ..." (Job 7:18).

You are so valuable to the Lord and He magnifies you to this realm where He comes down from heaven to visit with you every morning. Most of the time when He visits you are asleep, but because of His extreme kindness, He gives dreams so He can still *visit* most believers in the morning. However, it is far better to be up and waiting in prayer for His visitation!

You must understand that a visitation from the Lord is Him making a special trip, it is not that He comes and stays. A visit is like if your Aunt or another relative visits your family once a year, they stay for a time and then leave. Every time the Lord visits the earth He only comes for a certain amount of time and then He's gone. That is why He told me He missed the time we spent together in the morning. When you get this understanding, you can tap into the blessings of the morning time visitation!

He Seeks You in the Morning

*"And why dost thou not pardon my transgression, and take away mine iniquity? for now shall I sleep in the dust; and **thou shalt seek me in the morning, but I shall not be,"*** (Job 7:21).

This scripture proves that God does indeed get off His throne every morning and come down to the earth to visit you. Job said, ***"thou shalt seek me in the morning,** but I shall not be,"* he knew the power of morning prayer and woke up early to intercede for his family because he also knew that God visited the earth every morning (Job 1:5). Job was going through a lot of trials, he lost his businesses and his children, Satan plagued Job with painful boils all over his body, and then he felt that death was closing in on him. He said, *"Lord, if I die, when you come on earth in the morning and look for me to spend time with me I will not be here."* (Job 7:21). In this scripture, Job verified that God comes on earth every morning to seek for us. He asked God to forgive his sins and deliver him from the grievous affliction he was experiencing, and if He did not, He would not find him in the morning.

Every time I read this scripture it amazes me. Many saints miss the point because they do not understand the true meaning of prayer. They don't understand that prayer is fellowship with God. I get up because I know He's on earth and that He's looking for me. He's looking for you too!

God Visits Adam in the Cool of the Day

"For I am the LORD, I change not; therefore ye sons of Jacob are not consumed," (Malachi 3:6). God does not change, He is the same yesterday, today, and forever. What He did at the beginning with Adam

He is still doing today! Adam's sin did not keep God from visiting man every morning. He did not change His routine because man changed. The Bible says, **"And they heard the voice of the LORD God walking in the garden in the cool of the day:** *and Adam and his wife hid themselves from the presence of the LORD God amongst the trees of the garden,"* (Genesis 3:8).

"The voice of the LORD God walking in the garden," are tragic words, because before Adam sinned, he had a face to face relationship with God and spoke with Him mouth to mouth. After he sinned, Adam could only hear God's voice. A voice does not walk, a person does. However, the Bible specifically mentions the voice walking. You must understand God cannot be separated from His voice. When Elijah waited on Mount Horeb for God to come down, the Bible says,

"And, behold, the LORD passed by, and a great and strong wind rent the mountains, and brake in pieces the rocks before the LORD; but the LORD was not in the wind: and after the wind an earthquake; but the LORD was not in the earthquake: ***And after the earthquake a fire; but the LORD was not in the fire: and after the fire a still small voice.*** *And it was so, when Elijah heard it, that he wrapped his face in his mantle, and went out, and stood in the entering in of the cave..."* (1 Kings 19:11-13).

Do you see how God was not in the wind nor in the earthquake nor in the fire? Elijah did not move out of the cave until he heard the **"still small voice"** of God. When you read about the voice of God walking in the garden, you must understand that God's person was physically walking there. However, because of the fall, Adam could not see Him.

"But your iniquities have separated between you and your God, **and your sins have hid his face from you,** *that he will not hear,"* (Isaiah 59:2). It was man's sin condition that hid God's face because the wages of sin are death. Adam would have died if he saw God in his sinful condition, therefore, <u>God hid His face to save man's life. Before Adam sinned, the Father, Son, and the Holy Spirit appeared to him in the garden every morning.</u> Many think that there is death in God's

The Importance of the Watch and God's Visit

face because of what God said to Moses when he asked to see His glory.

> *"And he said, Thou canst not see my face: for there shall no man see me, and live,"* (Exodus 33:20).

These words are also tragic, and preachers constantly use this scripture wrongly when they say, *"No man can see God's face."* When I preach and teach that you can have a face to face relationship with the Lord, these preachers say, *"All of you that are talking about seeing Jesus or that you can see God, are wrong, it is not scriptural. You know no man can see God and live."* Sadly, they quote these scriptures out of immaturity and ignorance, not out of revelation. Remember, before sin came into the world, man could see God. When God formed man from the dirt, He **"breathed into his nostrils the breath of life; and man became a living soul,"** (Genesis 2:7). God literally gave man CPR when He breathed life into his nostrils! When a person drowns and is given CPR, the first person he or she sees, is the person doing the CPR. When Adam woke up for the first time, he was looking in God's face. In the beginning, man was face to face with God!

You must understand that God made us for relationship, fellowship, intimacy, and communion. He made us in His own image and likeness so that He could fellowship with us. Before Adam sinned, we could fully experience God, see His face, and live in His countenance.

> *"Wherefore, **as by one man sin entered into the world, and death by sin;** and so death passed upon all men, for that all have sinned,"* (Romans 5:12).

When Adam sinned, he lost the intimacy and direct contact relationship he once had with God.

Jesus Came to Restore Our First Love: Face to Face with God

Since Jesus died to save man from sin, the veil has been removed, and we can see God face to face again! Isn't that wonderful and glorious? Jesus shed His Blood and dealt with the sin that destroyed

THE WINGS OF THE MORNING

our relationship with the Father. The Bible says, *"To wit, that **God was in Christ, reconciling the world unto himself,** not imputing their trespasses unto them..."* (2 Corinthians 5:19). Jesus started restoring things we lost and said to His disciples, *"... neither knoweth any man the Father, save the Son and He to whomsoever the Son will reveal him,"* (Matthew 11:27). Jesus came to reveal or unveil the Father to "whomsoever" He wants to!

> *"He that hath my commandments, and keepeth them, he it is that loveth me: and he that loveth me shall be loved of my Father, and **I will love him, and will manifest myself to him,**"* (John 14:21).

Jesus spoke about manifesting Himself to those who love Him. That word manifest in the Greek means to show oneself in person, or to make an appearance. It also means to disclose oneself by words. An appearance is therefore manifested in two dimensions. The first dimension is when the Lord comes and shows His face to you, and it is the highest realm of the face to face relationship with the Godhead. The second dimension is when the Lord comes to you and discloses Himself by words. Just because you only hear the voice and do not see His face, does not mean He is not standing there. He is disclosing Himself to you in an appearance by words. Samuel experienced an appearance by words, *"**And the LORD came, and stood, and called** as at other times, Samuel, Samuel. Then Samuel answered, Speak; for thy servant heareth,"* (1 Samuel 3:10).

The Lord appeared to Samuel when he was just a little child and continued to reveal Himself by words as Samuel grew. *"**And the LORD appeared again in Shiloh: for the LORD revealed himself to Samuel in Shiloh by the word of the LORD,**"* (1 Samuel 3:21). Hearing the Word of God without seeing Him is also an appearance! God can stand beside you in the morning time visitation prayer and talk to you, and even though you do not see Him, this scripture confirms that He is there.

Have you ever been asleep and heard the Lord speaking words to you in your sleep, then you woke up? He was standing in that room with you even if you were asleep. Most of the time this happens in the morning because He is on earth. He never misses this visitation. We should be experiencing even more than the ancient saints did because

Jesus Christ brought better things to our dispensation when He shed His Blood to redeem us and to bring restitution to all things. You should be hearing God speak when He visits you in the morning and you should be seeing Him face to face! With the Keys of the Kingdom of God, I release all these dimensions of face to face appearances from the Lord in your life in Jesus' name!

> *"And when the sabbath was past, Mary Magdalene, and Mary the mother of James, and Salome, had bought sweet spices, that they might come and anoint him.* ***And very early in the morning the first day of the week, they came unto the sepulchre at the rising of the sun,"*** (Mark 16:1-2).

> *"The first day of the week* ***cometh Mary Magdalene early, when it was yet dark,*** *unto the sepulchre, and seeth the stone taken away from the sepulchre,"* (John 20:1).

People all over the world celebrate the resurrection of Jesus. Did you know that God raised Him early in the morning? In Mark, it says that the women set out to the tomb "very early in the morning," Matthew reveals that the women got to the tomb ***"... as it began to dawn toward the first day of the week...,"*** John says the women came while it was still dark outside, and we know that when they got to the tomb Jesus was not there! He was risen from the dead very early in the morning! Everything God does is significant. He could have raised Jesus at any time of the day, but He did it in the morning, because He routinely visits the earth early every morning. *"Him God raised up the third day, and shewed him openly"* (Acts 10:40). Jesus did not get up from the grave on His own. Jehovah was on earth and He went to the tomb and raised Jesus by His eternal Spirit. <u>No matter what is dead in your life, if you get up to meet God when He visits, He will resurrect it!</u>

You Visit God vs Him Visiting You

One time during prayer I said, *"Lord, why is it that the morning is so significant?"* He said, *"I chose to do things that way."* He explained that whenever someone gets up to pray at noon or in the evening, it is them appearing before or visiting God. ***"Let us therefore come boldly unto the throne of grace,*** *that we may obtain mercy, and find grace to help in time of* *need"* (Hebrews 4:16). You have the right and ability to go before the throne of God whenever you want to.

> *"My soul thirsteth for God, for the living God:* **when shall I come and appear before God?"** (Psalm 42:2).

David loved visiting with God. He could not wait to run into the Tent of God to meet with Him every day. He knew what it took to go up the hill of the Lord. *"Who shall ascend into the hill of the LORD? or who shall stand in his holy place? He that hath clean hands, and a pure heart..."* (Psalm 24:3-4). The "key of David" is praise and worship and caused him to ascend into the courts of the Lord. *"Serve the LORD with gladness:* **come before his presence with singing. Enter into his gates with thanksgiving, and into his courts with praise..."** (Psalm 100:2,4). Through praise, you can get God to visit you because He inhabits the praises of His people (Psalm 22:3).

There is a major difference in you visiting the Lord and Him visiting you. You cannot expect the Lord to visit you at noon or evening unless He chooses to or you invite Him with worship. Jesus told the woman at the well that God seeks those who worship Him in spirit and in truth. When you start to get deep into worship you begin to feel the intense presence of the Lord, and that is great, but I am emphasizing and explaining that His schedule is in the morning.

The Lord said to me, *"You know, David, you can choose to get up and pray to me on your time. That is wonderful and I will hear you, but that is you visiting me. When you visit me on your time your spirit can only be open to what you really need and want at that time. It cannot be open to anything I want to do because it is not My visit with you, and you are out of timing to be open to what I want."*

When the Lord revealed the true significance of the morning time visitation, I began to understand why Jesus said, *"I miss the times we used to spend together in the mornings."*

When you get up early in the morning to meet with Him, He is visiting with you. When God visits you, it is not necessarily about what you want to talk about, but <u>what He wants to address and talk about</u>. Most of the time, believers pray to God on their time, not His. Your spirit cannot be open to what God wants to do with you every day if you do not get up in the morning to meet with Him. Missing God's morning visitation, causes you to be off in your timing, off-centered, and therefore you miss the things He planned for you.

    The Lord is so merciful, He will bring you back around, it just takes longer. Meet Him when He is on earth and your whole life will get into balance. He will start putting things on your heart that He wants to discuss with you, that you won't get unless you get up in the morning. You can get revelations by studying or by praying and fasting but there are certain revelations that God will never give you because you are not in the right timing and your mind and spirit are not open to receive when He is n earth in the morning.

CHAPTER 3
Discerning Visitations

CHAPTER 3
Discerning Visitations

Laws Governing Visitations

You must understand the laws governing visitations so you can get the most out of them. When the Lord comes down, He is visiting, and making a special trip to meet you and you must catch the moment. In every visitation, whether it is a visitation from God to a city, a person, or a church, He has a purpose to give you something. If you miss it, you miss the blessings, and the things that belong to your peace in that season. God can redeem time and return to you later, but you must realize that there are different visitations, and each one carries blessings and judgments.

Some might say, *"Wait a minute! God is omnipresent. He is everywhere so we can access him anytime and anywhere. Why do you say the morning time is the only time I can expect God to visit me every day?"* Yes, God is omnipresent because He fills the whole universe. His very presence preserves our existence. *"For in him we live, and move, and have our being,"* (Acts 17:28). *"For he hath said, I will never leave thee, nor forsake thee,"* (Hebrews 13:5). God is always with you, everywhere you go. *"Whither shall I go from thy spirit? or whither shall I flee from thy presence?"* (Psalm 139:7). David explains that not even Heaven, Hell, or the sea can hide you from God's presence.

You must understand the difference between God's presence and His person. When He visits in the morning, it is not only His presence, His person is physically on earth, and you must understand how major it is. Jehovah God and an entourage of angels were physically on the earth every morning with Adam and Eve. That's why that angel who wrestled with Jacob said, *"Let me go, for the day breaketh,"* (Genesis 32:26). Time was up for the angel he had to go back with God.

Knowing the Time of Your Visitation

*"Saying, **If thou hadst known, even thou, at least in this thy day, the things which belong unto thy peace! but now they are hid from thine eyes.** For the days shall come upon thee, that thine enemies shall cast a trench about thee, and compass thee round, and keep thee in on every side, And shall lay thee even with the ground, and thy children within thee; and they shall not leave in thee one stone upon another; **because thou knewest not the time of thy visitation,"*** (Luke 19:42-44).

The rule of law concerning every visitation is that when God comes to you there is something that He wants to accomplish and something He wants to give you. With every visitation from the Lord, you must have knowledge of what He is granting you, because there are things that belong to you in that visitation that you may not get in other ones. The Bible says that not knowing the time of your visitation allows your enemy to come against you,

*"And shall lay thee even with the ground, **and thy children within thee;** and they shall not leave in thee one stone upon another; **because thou knewest not the time of thy visitation,"*** (Luke 19:44).

If you do not know the time of your visitation you will miss things and even your children will be affected. There are two laws of visitation that you must know.

> **Number 1**: You must know the time that God is going to visit you because, *"To every thing there is a season, and a time to every purpose under the heaven,"* (Ecclesiastes 3:1). God channels everything He does through time, including His visitations. Therefore, you must have wisdom and study about God's timing. (Ecclesiastes 8:5).

Discerning Visitations

Number 2: You must know the things that belong to you and what god wants to give you. *"Saying, If thou hadst known, even thou, at least in this thy day, the things which belong unto thy peace! but now they are hid from thine eyes"* (Luke 19:42). We are not to be ignorant about the things that will bring us peace when we have visitations today. Ignorance cuts you off from the life of God and denies access to the things that belong to your peace.

It is not enough to know the time of your visitation from the Lord, you must also know the things that belong to your peace in that visitation. If you struggle and fight to make things happen, it can be an indication that you are ignorant and do not understand the time of your visitation. When God comes to you, things that would take you 20 years to do, He can do in a month, two days, or even in a moment. Visitations shorten the length of time and the struggle you would normally go through to make things happen.

"Thou hast granted me life and favour, and thy visitation hath preserved my spirit," (Job 10:12). In visitations there is life, favor, and preservation! *"O visit me with thy salvation,"* (Psalm 106:4). When He visits you in the morning time He waters and enriches your life (Psalm 65:9). These are just a few of the things that belong to your peace when He visits your life.

The Messianic Visitation

2000 years ago, God visited the earth specifically through Jesus for a reason. For many years and generations, this visitation was prophesied by the Law and the Prophets. The Jews were in great expectation for the Messiah to come and save them, but when He came, they missed it. The Jewish nation rejected Him and missed everything that came with that visitation and were severely judged. Their enemies came against them and laid them to the ground, and the Kingdom of God that was entrusted to them was taken and delivered to the Gentile nations because they missed the time of their visitation.

In the gospels, Jesus gave knowledge concerning the things He was bringing in this specific visitation. He was sent from heaven to earth to save people from their sins. The angel of the Lord appeared to Joseph concerning the child Mary was carrying and said to him, *"... **call his name JESUS: for he shall save his people from their sins,** "* (Matthew 1:21). The Jews missed their salvation when they rejected Him, they were destroyed by the Romans, and they lost their peace! When you miss the time of your visitation you miss what Jesus is bringing in that visitation. <u>When you get knowledge of the visitation, you can cooperate with Him better, and access all its blessings.</u>

Zechariah, the father of John, gave a key prophecy about Christ's visitation to the Jews, **"To give knowledge of salvation unto his people by the remission of their sins**, *Through the tender mercy of our God; whereby the* **dayspring from on high hath visited us,** *To give light to them that sit in darkness and in the shadow of death, to guide our feet into the way of peace,"* (Luke 1:77-79).

The Messianic visitation brought "knowledge of salvation" to the Jews. If they understood and received the visitation, they would have received remission of sins. Zechariah mentioned that Jesus, as the Dayspring from on high, *"hath visited us."* Christ coming to the earth was a visitation of light and deliverance to those who were bound in darkness and in the shadow of death. Zechariah also confirmed that Christ's visit to the earth was to guide the Jews *"into the way of peace,"* (Luke 1:79). Israel would have experienced peace if they received Christ. *"...If thou hadst known, even thou, at least in this thy day,* **the things which belong unto thy peace!"** (Luke 19:42) However, they rejected Jesus and experienced war!

> *"For the days shall come upon thee, that* **thine enemies shall cast a trench about thee, and compass thee round, and keep thee in on every side,** *And shall lay thee even with the ground, and thy children within thee; and they shall not leave in thee one stone upon another; because thou knewest not the time of thy visitation,"* (Luke 19:43-44).

Because the Jews did not know the things that belonged to them in that Messianic Visitation, they became spiritually blind. *"... but now they are hid from thine eyes,"* (Luke 19:42). When you miss your visitation, you become blind to what God was bringing to you, you are closed off to the blessings of that visitation. The whole nation of Israel became spiritually blind when they rejected the visitation of God through Christ Jesus. They missed their timing, and the Lord went to someone else (Matthew 21:43).

There were seasons when God visited and prompted me to fast and pray and told me how important each specific fast is to my life. When I did not fast and pray as He told me, my eyes got dim and I said, *"Oh well I can wait till the next time. It's not that bad. It's not that serious."* That thinking is what the Bible calls blindness. Many don't realize the seriousness and severe consequences of missing their visitation. Therefore, you must do what God tells you *when* He tells you to. When God tells you to make changes in your life about things you know are wrong, such as being in ungodly relationships, and you don't, it gets harder, because after God tells you to do a thing the next one to come is Satan and he is going to make it hard for you to change.

The Enemy Comes If You Miss Your Visitation

"For the days shall come upon thee, that thine enemies shall cast a trench about thee, and compass thee round, and keep thee in on every side," (Luke 19:43).

When Israel missed the Messianic Visitation, they experienced war with the Romans, who were their enemy, and they were destroyed. Whenever you miss God's visitation, the opposite of what you should receive happens. If you miss the rapture you will miss meeting the Lord in the clouds, the Antichrist will come, and you will experience great tribulation.

When God starts visiting you and tells you to do something, if you don't do it when He tells you to, something bad happens because you cannot do anything in your strength. *"... for without me ye can do nothing,"* (John 15:5). When the Lord tells you to do something, do it then, or you lose the grace to do it!

When people say, *"I'll get saved when I get ready,"* often run out of opportunities to get saved. You cannot come to God on your terms, you must come when He's drawing you, because He releases grace for you to do it. *"For by grace are ye saved through faith; and that not of yourselves: it is the gift of God,"* (Ephesians 2:8). You do not know when the Lord will cycle back to you, so respond when He is drawing you.

When you have an appointment with God to pray, and miss it, the enemy comes, *"And ye yourselves like unto men that wait for their lord, when he will return from the wedding; that when he cometh and knocketh, they may open unto him immediately.* **Blessed are those servants, whom the lord when he cometh shall find watching:** *verily I say unto you, that he shall gird himself, and make them to sit down to meat, and will come forth and serve them. And if he shall come in the second watch, or come in the third watch, and find them so, blessed are those servants. And this know, that* **if the goodman of the house had known what hour the thief would come, he would have watched, and not have suffered his house to be broken through,"** (Luke 12:36-39).

Jesus blesses those He finds on their watch praying and waiting on Him! *"Blessed are those servants, whom the lord when he cometh shall find watching."* When you do not miss your time of prayer, the Lord serves you with whatever you need in that season of your life Himself, but if you miss your time the thief breaks into your house and you lose major things in your life. *"So shall thy poverty come as one that travelleth; and thy want as an armed man,"* (Proverbs 24:34). It is disastrous not to watch and pray and to miss your visitation.

The Rapture Visitation

"For the Lord himself shall descend from heaven with a shout, with the voice of the archangel, and with the trump of God: and the dead in Christ shall rise first: **Then we which are alive and remain shall be caught up together with them in the clouds, to meet the Lord in the air:** *and so shall we ever be with the Lord,"* (1 Thessalonians 4:16-17).

Another visitation is known in the church as the Rapture, the return of the Lord's visitation. When you have knowledge of this visitation, you will be among those that are translated with Jesus in the clouds and go to heaven to be with Him. If you miss this visitation, by not being ready when Jesus comes back, you will be left here with the

Antichrist. The knowledge of the Rapture visitation is that Jesus is coming again to get us out of the earth.

*"**And take heed to yourselves, lest at any time** your hearts be overcharged with surfeiting, and drunkenness, and cares of this life, **and so that day come upon you unawares.** For as a snare shall it come on all them that dwell on the face of the whole earth. **Watch ye therefore, and pray always, that ye may be accounted worthy to escape all these things that shall come to pass, and to stand before the Son of man,"*** (Luke 21:34-36).

This is the knowledge of what belongs to your peace in the Rapture Visitation. Jesus commands us to "take heed" that we are not distracted, unaware, by the cares and things of this world. Not being careful and vigilant will cause you to miss the visitation and everything that comes with it. Jesus also talks about what you need to do to be ready for His return. We must watch and pray so we escape the torment the rest of the world will experience. This is the knowledge and intricate details of what belongs to your peace in the Rapture visitation.

What you receive during the morning time visitation is different from what you receive in the rapture visitation. When the Lord comes every morning to visit the earth, He is not taking us back on the clouds with Him. The Rapture is a day that no one knows. However, clues and indications for the people of God are found in Matthew 24, Mark 14, and Luke 21:7-36. Study those passages and you will know what belongs to you and what to do so you won't miss it. ***"And when these things begin to come to pass, then look up,*** *and lift up your heads; for your redemption draweth nigh,"* (Luke 21:28). We may not know the day or the hour, but we can tell the season of Jesus' return by the signs He laid out in the gospels.

The Temple Visitation

Malachi spoke of the Temple Visitation, *"Behold, I will send my messenger, and he shall prepare the way before me:* ***and the Lord, whom ye seek, shall suddenly come to his temple,*** *even the messenger of the covenant,* *whom ye delight in: behold, he shall come, saith the LORD of hosts,"* (Malachi 3:1).

The messenger of the covenant will come *suddenly* to His temple. Have you ever been in a service when the presence of God floods the church and you see people crying, falling under the power, getting healed and delivered, and so on? What do you think happened? Jesus suddenly came into the temple and they received what belonged to their peace. Malachi tells us that Jesus comes to the temple like a refiner's fire and fullers' soap.

"But who may abide the day of his coming? ***and who shall stand when he appeareth?*** *for he is like a refiner's fire, and like fullers' soap:* ***And he shall sit as a refiner and purifier of silver: and he shall purify the sons of Levi,*** *and purge them as gold and silver, that they may offer unto the LORD an offering in righteousness,"* (Malachi 3:2-3).

When Jesus comes into the temple suddenly, condemnation, guilt, and sin, are washed away, and you feel so much better. He applies the detergent of the "fullers' soap" to your life sanctifying and cleansing you from all sin and upgrades your life and existence to a higher rank and dimension in Him. Through the process and refinement, you move from strength to strength, glory to glory, and grace to grace. Judgment and correction are also released when Jesus visits the temple.

"And I will come near to you to judgment; and I will be a swift witness *against the sorcerers, and against the adulterers, and against false swearers, and against those that oppress the hireling in his wages, the widow, and the fatherless, and that turn aside the stranger from his right, and fear not me, saith the LORD of hosts. For I am the LORD, I change not; therefore ye sons of Jacob are not consumed,"* (Malachi 3:5-6).

As He did during His earthly ministry, Jesus still brings judgment and correction to those who are out of the will and are rebels to the Kingdom, like He did when He whipped the money changers and the ones selling doves in the temple (Matthew 21:12-13). He becomes a swift witness against sorcerers and all workers of iniquity. When men and women of God are ministering, you may see them suddenly deal with things and people who are an offense to God, because it preserves the saints from being consumed or destroyed.

The amazing thing about the temple visitation is that God's eye and heart are perpetually established in the church. After He dedicated the Temple of Solomon He said, *"I have hallowed this house, which thou hast built, to put my name there for ever; and mine eyes and mine heart shall be there perpetually,"* (1 Kings 9:3). The temple is hallowed, sanctified, and a holy place, where God's eyes and heart are situated, that is why you feel His presence in churches where He is Lord. You must understand that when He visits the temple, it is an actual manifestation of His person and it happens every time the people gather to worship God.

"For where two or three are gathered together in my name, there am I in the midst of them," (Matthew 18:20).

Whenever two or more believers gather in the name of Jesus, the Lord physically manifests there and whatever you agree on is granted because the temple is primarily a house of prayer. When the Lord is in the midst, amazing things happen and prayers are answered, because they belong to your peace in that visitation.

"Saying, I will declare thy name unto my brethren, **in the midst of the church will I sing praise unto thee,"** (Hebrews 2:12). In many church services there are moments when the presence and glory of God invade the temple because the praise and worship is right, and Jesus is there in person praising and worshipping the Father with you! <u>When you miss gathering together with the saints</u>, <u>you miss Jesus joining you.</u> Anything Jesus did in synagogues throughout the cities and villages of Israel, He does today! *"Jesus Christ the same yesterday, and to day, and for ever,"* (Hebrews 13:8).

Why People Miss the Morning Visitation
The Invisible Father Operates Best in the Secret Realm

There are multiple things that the Father does when He comes to the earth every morning. However, many saints miss Him because of how He visits the earth. God is so humble, meek, and gentle, you have no idea that He's even on the earth unless you study His visitations like you are now. He does His work in the meekness of wisdom, therefore, you must know what to look for to even discern that He's visiting you. God operates in the invisible realm in a mild and meek manner. *"Verily thou art a God that hidest thyself, O God of Israel, the Saviour,"* (Isaiah 45:15). God does His best works in secret and rewards those who understand the secret place of prayer. When you understand this mystery, you will reap the rewards of the fourth watch visitation.

When God comes on earth every morning, He does not make a grand entrance with thunder, lightning, and booming voices, shaking and quaking to wake everyone up. His meekness, quiet, and secret way of coming does not mean that He is not there.

*"But thou, when thou prayest, enter into thy closet, and when thou hast shut thy door, pray to thy **Father which is in secret; and thy Father which seeth in secret** shall reward thee openly,"* (Matthew 6:6).

The Father does things in such a secret, hidden, and invisible way that if you are not discerning, you will miss what He did when He visited the earth. When you met Him at 3 a.m., He was physically with you, and you received a dispensation of grace that, at the appropriate time, will manifest openly! *"For there is nothing hid, which shall not be manifested; neither was any thing kept secret, but that it should come abroad,"* (Mark 4:22).

The price for open rewards is meeting God in the secret place when He comes to earth. *"What I tell you in darkness, that speak ye in light: and what ye hear in the ear, that preach ye upon the housetops"* (Matthew 10:27). When you meet God in secret you will have an open manifestation that you can preach or proclaim publicly.

Knowing What Belongs to Your Peace in the Morning Visitation

As previously mentioned, one of the blessings that comes from morning visitations is that God gives you wings to move faster and catch up in the areas you are behind. Meeting Him in the morning accelerates your destiny.

God does different things at different times of the day. Therefore, you cannot immerse or throw all times of prayer into the same pot and say, *"I can pray at any time and God will hear me."* While that is true, having that mindset can undermine the specific and special things God wants to do in your life and can only be accessed during the morning visitation.

If you do not know and understand what the Lord is there to do, you will miss everything He brings with Him. You must get knowledge and understanding! ***"If thou hadst known, even thou, at least in this thy day, the things which belong unto thy peace!*** *but now they are hid from thine eyes,"* (Luke 19:42).

The morning visitations carry great weight with God, due to sheer volume and frequency, He comes every single morning and brings something critical for your life and destiny. God gives certain things and measures in the morning visitation that He does not give at any other time of the day, and this book covers many of them.

CHAPTER 4
Forty Benefits of Fourth Watch Prayer

CHAPTER 4
Forty Benefits of Fourth Watch Prayer

Rewards of Morning Time Visitations

God has chosen a window of time to release Himself on the earth, from 3 a.m. until the breaking of day. When you wake up early to meet Him at that time, you are meeting the best person you could ever meet, at the right time. Many blessings come with Him! I found several places in scripture that spoke of the things God does for us in the morning visitations. One blessing is: *"They are new every morning: great is Thy faithfulness,"* (Lamentations 3:23). Here are a few more things that belong to your peace in the morning time visitation:

1. He brings His justice to light every morning (Zephaniah 3:5).

2. New are His mercies every morning (Lamentations 3:22-23).

3. He promises to waken you morning by morning (Isaiah 50:4).

4. He promises to waken your spiritual ear to hear as the learned. This is the ear of the learned. He opens our ears every morning to hear Him spiritually (Isaiah 50:4-5). This learning also keeps us out of rebellion and from turning our back on Him (Psalm 143:8). When you wake up in the morning be expecting to hear from God (Psalm 92:2).

5. He gives us the tongue of the learned (Isaiah 50:4).

6. You receive quicker transportation from God spiritually, "the wings of the morning" (Psalm 139:9).

7. He comes seeking and looking for us by a personal visit every morning (Job 7:18,21 and Genesis 3:8).

8. He comes walking in the cool of the day, the mornings (Genesis 3:8; Hosea 6:3).

9. God's power and glory are shown to us (Psalm 63:1-2; Exodus 33; 34:1-8).

10. Your nature and character of rebellion against God are changed by Him. He gives you another name as He did Jacob (Genesis 32:24-28).

11. Your prayers will prevail with God at this time (Genesis 32:24-28; Job 8:6).

12. He promises that you will get His attention. He will wake up for you (Job 8:5-6).

13. He promises to make the habitation of your righteousness prosperous (Job 8:6).

14. He promises to enlarge your latter end greatly. He promises to turn your small beginning into a big end (Job 8:7).

15. He promises that joy will come (Psalm 30:5). The joy of His way comes (Job 8:19,21). He rejoices over us with joy through singing to us (Zephaniah 3:17).

16. He promises to send a prophet to you with a message or a prophetic message in the morning in some way (2 Samuel 24:11-12).

17. Seeds miraculously grow and flourish (Psalm 90:6; Ecclesiastes 11:6).

18. You receive power and dominion from God (Genesis 32:24-28; Psalm 49:14).

Forty Benefits of Fourth Watch Prayer

19. God commands the morning (Job 38:12).

20. The morning is a womb (Psalm 110:3).

21. You receive the spiritual inheritance of spiritual fathers (Job 8:7-10).

22. A Blessing is pronounced on you in the morning (Genesis 32:26-29).

23. You receive the royal power of a prince in the morning (Genesis 32:28).

24. Power with God comes in the morning. He comes and works directly with you and through you (Genesis 32:28).

25. Power and favor with Men comes in the morning (Genesis 32:28).

26. God shows His loving kindness in the morning (Psalm 92:2). He commands His lovingkindness in the daytime (Psalm 42:8) but manifests it during the morning time visitation.

27. You receive discernment to choose a staff (Luke 6:12-16).

28. God fights for you in the morning (Exodus 14:24-25). (Exodus 10:13; 1 Sam 11:11; Job 24:17).

29. You will find wisdom when you seek her early in the morning (Proverbs 8:17).

30. You receive power to cast off the works of darkness at daybreak (Romans 13:11-12).

31. Kings are like the light of the morning (2 Samuel 23:4). That means God's divine kings are morning people like God and Jesus (Job 7:18; Hosea 6:3).

32. Bread, manna, and the Word of God come in the morning (Exodus 16:8,12-13; Luke 21:38; John 8:2 Acts 5:21).

THE WINGS OF THE MORNING

33. Appearances from the Lord (Exodus 16:7; Exodus 19:16; John 21:4).

34. Incense representing prayer is offered in the morning (Exodus 30:7; Psalm 5:3; 88:13; Psalm 141:2; Mark 1:35).

35. The fourth watch is the best time to seek God because He goes forth and visits the earth in the morning (Job 7:18; Hosea 5:15; 6:3; Isaiah 55:6).

36. You receive God's help in the morning (Psalm 46:5).

37. God satisfies you with His mercy early in the morning (Psalm 90:14).

38. Those who diligently seek the Lord in the fourth watch obtain God's favor and they are a delight to Him (Proverbs 11:27).

39. Seek God early in the morning when you are in trouble, afflicted, and oppressed and He will heal you, bind you up, revive and raise you up (Hosea 5:15; Hosea 6:1-2).

40. Your spirit is stirred up to seek God early in the morning (Isaiah 26:9).

These blessings belong to your peace in the morning time visitation prayer. *"My people are destroyed for lack of knowledge: because thou hast rejected knowledge, I will also reject thee ..."* (Hosea 4:6). You need knowledge of what belongs to your peace so that you will not be destroyed. God does not want us to be ignorant of what brings us peace, pursue the knowledge of these blessings and receive them today!

CHAPTER 5
The Mercies of Fourth Watch

CHAPTER 5
The Mercies of Fourth Watch

New Mercies Belong to Your Peace in the Morning

*"**It is of the LORD'S mercies** that we are not consumed, because his compassions fail not. **They are new every morning:** great is thy faithfulness,"* (Lamentations 3:22-23).

One thing that belongs to you in the morning is new mercies. Mercy is the pity and consideration of God for your life and is a major blessing of morning prayer. We have heard, quoted, and sang songs about this scripture for so long, but the church at large does not know the depth of what it means. After the Lord revealed the significance of morning visitations to me, I studied and searched the scriptures to find everything that belongs to me in the morning time visitation, and when I came across this verse, the Lord said to me, *"David my people think they get new mercies every day. That is the way it's been interpreted in the Body of Christ, but it is wrong. I give new mercies every morning, but you must get up to meet me to receive them."*

God said His mercies *"are new every morning,"* and are given faithfully and without fail, when He comes to earth every morning. *"...* ***great is thy faithfulness,"*** however, if you miss the morning visitation you miss the new mercies too. They belong to you when you meet Him to obtain them.

*"Let us therefore come boldly unto the throne of grace, **that we may obtain mercy,** and find grace to help in time of need,"* (Hebrews 4:16).

If we must go to the throne of God to obtain mercy, you need to understand that new mercies don't come to you, just because morning arrived. I used to think new mercies were mine just because the Bible says they are new every morning. Mercy has to be obtained it is not just given to you. *"Blessed are the merciful: **for they shall obtain mercy,"*** (Matthew 5:7). You must rise early in the morning and meet God to obtain new mercies, because they have a lifestyle of getting up early in the morning to pray. I have also noticed a strong supernatural presence in people who practice morning visitation prayer, by meeting God when He is on earth.

Defining New Mercies

*"**It is of the LORD'S mercies** that we are not consumed ... They are new every morning,"* (Lamentations 3:22-23).

The word new means fresh, a new thing, to rebuild, renew, and to repair. Every morning when God comes on earth with new mercies, He is coming to rebuild you and restore all the broken areas of your life, ensuring that any damaged or broken-down area is repaired and restructured! How glorious to know that this belongs to your peace every single morning!

It is because of the Lord's mercies *"that we are not consumed."* That word consumed means to make an end, to cease, to waste, to make a full end. In other words, every morning God's mercies keep whatever is attacking you from bringing a full end to your destiny, ministry, or life. As a believer, you go through many afflictions, trials, and tribulations, and without new mercies, you will never complete your assignment in life. However, in the morning visitation, God's mercies ensure that you are not consumed!

When you get up in the morning you don't just get yesterday's mercies, you get new ones, different from any other mercies you have already received. There are the sure mercies of David, salvation mercies, forgiveness mercies, traveling mercies, repentance mercies, etc., these mercies are already established in the Bible, and available to us right now. Yet, in His abundant mercy, God says, *"If you rise up at 3 a.m. to meet me during morning prayer time, I will keep making new mercies with you,"* mercies that are not even known yet!

Mercies operate like miracles because miracles, unlike healings, can be formed to resolve any situations in any realm. If you are in a building that is about to cave in, you need a miracle, not a healing. Just as there are diverse miracles, there are mercies for any kind of circumstance, and you need new mercies daily because you face problems that you didn't face yesterday.

God creates different kinds of mercy to meet each need, no matter the circumstance. For example, you need traveling mercies when you are on the highway and may be unaware that something on your car is broken and is setting you up to die in a wreck, but if you wake up early, you can obtain mercy and God will devise a way to keep that wreck from happening.

God knows how your day will go and He knows what new mercies He needs to formulate for you. Let me give you an example of how God is already doing this in your life without you even realizing it. Have you ever gotten up early in the morning and prayed, and even though bad things surrounded you, your whole day went very well? God still worked things out. Then there are days when you don't get up and meet God, things go bad, you experience a lack of favor, and negative things happen. If you get up and meet God, you obtain mercies, and even if Satan has planned attacks against you, they will be neutralized by God's mercy. It all comes out okay even when you are the problem, and it's your fault, because His new mercies still covered you. God is so wonderful to those who meet Him in the morning.

God Releases Multitudes of Mercies Every Morning

It is important to note that the scripture does not say "the Lord's mercy" it says, "the Lord's mercies," because there are so many mercies, and you need to start studying them to find out what belongs to you. God's Word mentions mercies many times.

*"Yet thou in thy **manifold mercies** forsookest them not in the wilderness,"* (Nehemiah 9:19).

*"Return, O LORD, deliver my soul: oh save me for **thy mercies'** sake,"* (Psalm 6:4).

*"Have mercy upon me, O God ... according unto the **multitude of thy tender mercies** blot out my transgressions,"* (Psalm 51:1).

*"... turn unto me according to the **multitude of thy tender mercies**,"* (Psalm 69:16).

*"And he ... repented according to the **multitude of his mercies**,"* (Psalm 106:45).

*"**... with great mercies will I gather thee**,"* (Isaiah 54:7).

*"Blessed be God ... **the Father of mercies**,"* (2 Corinthians 1:3).

God has a multitude of mercies, manifold mercies, great mercies, and He is the Father of mercies! One of the multitudes of mercies is dreams. For example, when Nebuchadnezzar was about to kill all the wise men of Babylon, Daniel asked for more time to get God's interpretation of the King's dream, *"**That they would desire mercies** of the God of heaven concerning this secret; that Daniel and his fellows should not perish with the rest of the wise men of Babylon,"* (Daniel 2:18).

Daniel and his friends asked for the mercies of God! They were asking God to pity and consider their lives by giving the interpretation to them and saving them from dying at the hands of the king. Through mercy, in a night vision, God gave Daniel the interpretation to the King's dream that saved their lives. When God gives you dreams with instructions and warnings, they are another manifestation of the multitude of His mercies, to protect and spare your life, and most of

The Mercies of Fourth Watch

these dreams or visions happen during the fourth watch (Job 33:14-18). There was an awesome man of God who had a huge and powerful ministry known all over the world. He planned on a vacation overseas. Shortly after he made his plans, someone on his staff had a dream that the plane crashed while the man was traveling, but when the staff member told the dream, the minister said, *"I rebuke that in Jesus' name. I believe in dreams, but I am going to bind that one,"* and he dismissed the dream. Another member of his staff members went to him and said, *"I feel like God is saying that you shouldn't go on this trip,"* and the minister bound that message as well. Because many leaders are the boss of their own ministry, they don't think they need to submit to anyone, and when God corrects them about something through another person, they find it hard to receive the rebuke. In His mercy, God gave another dream about his plane crashing, again, he would not listen. You must understand that there are things God tells us to do, not because we have authority to change them, but because He wants us to be obedient. There is a time to exercise authority over some things, and there is a time when you must submit to the Word of God, even if it comes through another person's dream.

Despite the warnings, the pastor went on vacation and during the night there was major turbulence, the plane crashed, and he died because he did not listen to the mercies of the Lord. Tragically and avoidably, he left behind a huge ministry. You must know the things that belong to your peace, so you do not suffer loss.

I remember when God warned me about people pulling guns on me, during a season when a lot of people that were in gangs were getting saved. When people pulled guns on me, and I knew they had devils in them, I rebuked and commanded them to give me the gun and they did. However, one day the Lord gave me a revelation and said, *"David, do you not know that when people tried to kill me, sometimes I ran and hid myself?"* In the gospels, there were several occasions when the Lord had to hide from the murderous intentions of the Jews and at times, He would not go to certain places because of it.

*"After these things Jesus walked in Galilee: **for he would not walk in Jewry, because the Jews sought to kill him,***" (John 7:1).

THE WINGS OF THE MORNING

Some people do not understand why Jesus, the only begotten Son of God, had to do that. When Jesus was a baby Herod tried to kill Him, and through a dream, God sent an angel to Joseph warning him to take Jesus and Mary and flee to Egypt. When Jesus was doing ministry there were times when He had to hide. Some say, *"Jesus the Son of God? The one who stopped the waves and sea, and walked on water? Why did HE have to run?"* If He was dealing with an evil spirit, He would simply rebuke and cast the demon out of a person, by the authority He had over demons. However, when a person decides to do something you need to be careful, because **God has given man free** will. *"But when they persecute you in this city, flee ye into another..."* (Matthew 10:23). The Apostles had to run and hide many times. It is important to heed God's instructions.

I realized what the Lord was saying, and in my crusades, I started to position certain men around, because the Lord showed me in a dream that someone would try to assassinate me. He instructed me to not let anybody walk up on me suddenly. Sometimes you can walk in authority to deal with certain situations but at other times you must have spiritual discernment and wisdom and put certain natural measures in place to avoid danger. There were times in Jesus' ministry when He rebuked the devils in certain violent men, and they were set free, and there were times when He ran away and hid Himself from evil people. That was wisdom.

> *"And when thy days be fulfilled, and thou shalt sleep with thy fathers, I will set up thy seed after thee, which shall proceed out of thy bowels, and I will establish his kingdom. He shall build an house for my name, and I will stablish the throne of his kingdom for ever. I will be his father, and he shall be my son. If he commit iniquity, I will chasten him with the rod of men, and with the stripes of the children of men:* **But my mercy shall not depart away from him, as I took it from Saul, whom I put away before thee.** *And thine house and thy kingdom shall be established for ever before thee:* **thy throne shall be established for ever,** *"* (2 Samuel 7:12-16).

Through the multitude of God's mercies, He promised an everlasting covenant, and the sure mercies of David, that he would be an eternal king and sit on a throne forever. David pioneered a new covenant of mercies with God because he understood morning time prayer and he was not consumed even when he made mistakes. God dealt differently with David than He did with Saul. *"But my mercy shall not depart away from him, as I took it from Saul, whom I put away before thee"* (2 Samuel 7:15). Because of the mercies David received every morning, his kingdom was preserved. Not so with Saul, his reign was completely ended, and his kingship was removed because he did not have the covenant of mercy.

> *"... I will make an everlasting covenant with you, even **the sure mercies of David**,"* (Isaiah 55:3).

The word "sure" means firm, stable, and permanent. In this scripture, God is telling Israel that He was going to give them the same covenant He gave David, but before could receive it, they would need to get up early. I want you to know that you can get up early in the morning and God will make this same covenant with you. If God made covenant with Israel many years after David died, He will make it with you through the Blood of Jesus today. Once you learn this covenant God made with David it will change your life like it has mine!

This covenant is not a natural one, it is an everlasting covenant of God's mercy, and even if you make a mistake, He will never move you! When God made this covenant with David He said, *"But my mercy shall not depart away from him, as I took it from Saul, whom I put away before thee"* (2 Samuel 7:15). Can you imagine God saying, "No matter what you do my mercy will never leave you!" He did it for David, and it covered his children as well. *"I will be his father, and he shall be my son: and I will not take my mercy away from him, as I took it from him that was before thee"* (1 Chronicles 17:13).

David's Kingship Preserved by Sure Mercies

*"For the king trusteth in the LORD, and **through the mercy of the most High he shall not be moved**,"* (Psalm 21:7).

By the mercy of God, David was not moved from his position and office as the King of Israel. *"If thou wouldest seek unto God betimes (early in the morning), and make thy supplication to the Almighty; If thou wert pure and upright; surely now he would awake for thee, and make the habitation of thy righteousness prosperous,"* (Job 8:5-6). If you rise and make your prayers and supplications in the morning time visitation prayer, God will turn things around through mercy and ensure that you are not removed from office as Saul was.

God did this for David not because David was beloved of the Lord, nor because he was more holy or righteous than Saul, it was because God gave David these sure mercies because of the covenant He had with him. Even when his son Absalom rebelled and tried to kill him, God protected David. Absalom got killed in the insurrection, because you cannot move someone that God has established, no matter what your opinion of them is. God will personally fight against those who oppose the people that are in covenant with Him!

"The enemy shall not exact upon him; nor the son of wickedness afflict him. And I will beat down his foes before his face, and plague them that hate him. But my faithfulness and my mercy shall be with him: and in my name shall his horn be exalted," (Psalm 89:22-24).

Part of the sure mercies covenant is that God fights anyone who comes against you and plagues people who hate you, therefore, it is reckless to come against anyone who has this covenant with God. There are different aspects, provisions, and terms connected to this covenant, and to come into the multitude of sure mercies you must search the Bible for everything God promised David and find what belongs to your peace. If you want this covenant, wake up early, because you only get sure mercies in the morning!

How I Received the Covenant of Sure Mercies

I remember a season when I was facing some of the worst persecution ever in ministry. I was constantly being criticized and ridiculed for the type of ministry I had, it got so bad, that I was discouraged. One night in a dream, Jesus showed a young lady to me and said, *"If you don't do this healing ministry, and stand at the forefront like Benny Hinn and Kathryn Kuhlman did in America, I will get a woman to do it."* I woke up out of that dream shaking and I said to the Lord, *"You don't have to find anybody, I will do your will!"*

I knew I needed to find a covenant that would cover me and prevent me from ever being moved from position. When God moved Saul, He told him through Samuel. *"... **The LORD hath rent the kingdom of Israel from thee this day, and hath given it to a neighbour of thine, that is better than thou,"*** (1 Samuel 15:28). God took the kingdom from Saul, and gave it to David, I did not want that to happen to me. I found the sure mercies of David, a realm in God where you can never be removed. *"For the king trusteth in the LORD, and through the mercy of the most High he shall not be moved,"* (Psalm 21:7). God said He wants to make this covenant with our generation. ***"... I will make an everlasting covenant with you, even the sure mercies of David"*** (Isaiah 55:3).

That does not mean that God will let you get away with doing evil things. When the Lord made this covenant with David, He said, *"I will be his father, and he shall be my son.* ***If he commit iniquity, I will chasten him with the rod of men, and with the stripes of the children of men: But my mercy shall not depart away from him,*** *as I took it from Saul, whom I put away before thee,"* (2 Samuel 7:14-15). Sometimes you go through certain persecutions and hardships because you did something wrong and God chastens you with the rod of men, through their wrong actions, but He promises that He will never remove His mercy from you, even in the midst of your wrong doings, because of the sure mercies of David.

If God gives you a position in His Kingdom and in the Body of Christ, you can ensure you never lose it, if you get up early in the morning and pray until daybreak. *"Therefore say I unto you, The kingdom of God shall be taken from you, and given to a nation bringing forth the fruits thereof,"* (Matthew 21:43). Israel was stripped of the kingdom for rejecting Jesus. I never want God to say anything like that to me. Imagine how hurtful it is for God to say He will remove you from your position with Him and give it to someone else because you are disobedient. God will protect your life and ministry with new mercies, now and in the future from certain disasters, if you get up, meet God, and pray in the morning.

The Blood of Jesus Gives You Access to All Covenants

God has given us access to walk in every covenant He made with Noah, Abraham, Isaac, Jacob, Moses, and anyone else in the Old Testament.

*"That at that time ye were without Christ, being aliens from the commonwealth of Israel, and strangers from the covenants of promise, having no hope, and without God in the world: **But now in Christ Jesus ye who sometimes were far off are made nigh by the blood of Christ,"*** (Ephesians 2:12-13).

Do you see how this scripture mentions that we were at one time strangers from the covenants of promise? The Blood of Jesus has given us access to all the covenants God made with Israel, Jesus paid the price for you to come into any covenant you can find in the Word of God.

How David Came into the Covenant of Sure Mercies

I have established that it is possible for you to come into this covenant God made with David, let me explain how it originated. God made this covenant when David expressed to Nathan the prophet that he wanted to build a temple for God. *"… See now, I dwell in an house of cedar, but the ark of God dwelleth within curtain,"* (2 Samuel 7:2). Even though Nathan endorsed David's desire and encouraged him to go ahead with his plan, God came and told Nathan to tell David that he would not be the one to build the temple, his son would, but because he desired to build it God said,

*"And when thy days be fulfilled, and thou shalt sleep with thy fathers, I will set up thy seed after thee, which shall proceed out of thy bowels, and I will establish his kingdom. He shall build an house for my name, and **I will Establish the throne of his kingdom for ever**. I will be his father, and he shall be my son. If he commit iniquity, I will chasten him with the rod of men, and with the stripes of the children of men: "But my mercy shall not depart away from him, as I took it from Saul, whom I put away before thee. And thine house and **thy kingdom shall be established for ever before thee: thy throne shall be established for ever,"*** (2 Samuel 7:13-16).

The Mercies of Fourth Watch

God established David's kingdom and throne forever, making him an eternal king. He assured David that He would not remove His mercy from him like He did Saul. God wanted to make Saul the first king of Israel, but he disobeyed God's commandments two times. I need you to understand that a King's throne and crown is established by obedience. Disobedience and rebellion to God's commands causes kings to lose their thrones. That is what happened to King Saul and God could not establish him eternally.

Saul's first act of disobedience happened when Samuel commanded that he wait for him, before performing a sacrifice, but the Philistine army was quickly advancing on Saul's army and he felt compelled to make the sacrifice himself. Immediately after Saul offered the sacrifice, Samuel appeared and said, *"... Thou hast done foolishly: thou hast not kept the commandment of the LORD thy God, which he commanded thee: for now would the LORD have established thy kingdom upon Israel for ever. But now thy kingdom shall not continue: the LORD hath sought him a man after his own heart, and the LORD hath commanded him to be captain over his people, because thou hast not kept that which the LORD commanded thee,"* (1 Samuel 13:13-14).

Because Saul did not keep the commandment and disobeyed God, he lost his kingdom. God gave him another chance to redeem himself and sent Saul to destroy the Amalekites, including all their livestock. However, he disobeyed God again when he spared King Agag of Amalek, only destroyed the weak and sickly livestock, and allowed his men to keep the healthy ones. God was greatly displeased and sent Samuel with this message to Saul, *"For rebellion is as the sin of witchcraft, and stubbornness is as iniquity and idolatry. Because thou hast rejected the word of the LORD, he hath also rejected thee from being king,"* (1 Samuel 15:23).

God rejected Saul as King of Israel because of his disobedience. Both his natural and eternal kingdoms were taken from him, and David replaced him as King of Israel. When God rejected Saul, He would not even speak to him through dreams. But through the sure mercies covenant, God promised David;

> *"But my mercy shall not depart away from him, as I took it from Saul, whom I put away before thee,"* (2 Samuel 7:15).

Why God Moved Saul but Established David

God rejected Saul from being King but assured David that he would never be removed. People today do not get this, because we know that David made some serious mistakes. He committed adultery with Bathsheba, the wife of Uriah the Hittite, then he had Uriah killed and married Bathsheba. When David did a national census without getting God's approval first, God plagued Israel and 70 thousand people were killed. However, despite making these mistakes, God remembered the covenant of salt that He made with David and he was not removed.

> *"Ought ye not to know that* **the LORD God of Israel gave the kingdom over Israel to David for ever, even to him and to his sons by a covenant of salt?"*
> (2 Chronicles 13:5).

A covenant of salt is irrevocable, because God established it on His own character, swearing by His own holiness to keep covenant with David, *"My covenant will I not break, nor alter the thing that is gone out of my lips.* **Once have I sworn by my holiness that I will not lie unto David.** *His seed shall endure for ever, and his throne as the sun before me"* (Psalm 89:34-36).

God would not reject or remove David, as he did Saul, even though he did terrible things, of which some would even argue, were worse than what Saul did. I used to say, *"Lord, it looks like David did worse than Saul. First, he took a man's wife and committed adultery with her, then he did not say or do anything for a for a whole year, and You did not remove David. Saul just didn't kill all the sheep like you told him to. There must be something wrong with this?!"* The Lord answered, *"David I do not judge like men do. It is one thing to sin against my holiness, but it is another thing to sin against my authority." "Behold, to obey is better than sacrifice..."* (1 Samuel 15:22). The kingly position is held by obedience to a command, not by weaknesses to the flesh and falling short of God's glory and holiness.

The Mercies of Fourth Watch

Then the Lord said to me, *"The difference in my judgment of Saul and David, is that David sinned against my holiness Saul directly disobeyed my authority. Sinning against my authority is rebellion and much worse than sinning against my holiness."* *"Whosoever therefore resisteth the power, resisteth the ordinance of God: and they that resist shall receive to themselves damnation"* (Romans 13:2). You receive damnation when you resist or sin against God's authority. It is one thing to sin against God's character and it is another thing entirely to sin against His authority.

When you sin against God's authority you are basically saying, *"I'm going to do what I want to do."* By his actions, that is what Saul did. Similarly, God moved Uzziah out of his position as a King and struck him with leprosy, because he disrespected rank and authority. (Uzziah moved out of position when he intruded into the priesthood office and tried to burn incense to God, in the day when kings were not anointed to be priests (2 Chronicles 26:16-21).

A king commands, and the moment he cannot obey a command, God removes him, because being a king deals with being obedient to God. You may not be perfect in your character, but you must learn to submit to and obey authority to be established in your kingship. Learning this caused me to understand why God removed His mercy from Saul, but preserved and promoted David, and will never take His sure mercies away from David or move him!

*"For the king trusteth in the LORD, and **through the mercy of the most High he shall not be moved,**"* (Psalm 21:7).

This mercy covers you even when you make mistakes like David did, but unlike Saul, David had a covenant of sure mercies with God. *"My mercy will I keep for him for evermore, and my covenant shall stand fast with him,"* (Psalm 89:28). Because Saul did not have this covenant, he was removed when he disobeyed God. It is vital that you understand having a *relationship* with God is more powerful than ministry. God fired Saul the day He rejected him but let him sit on the throne for the next 20 years. You must understand that God is so kind and meek, He will let you work even after He fires you, which is dangerous because many people are deceived by God's kindness.

David could stand on the promises of his covenant with God, and when he made one of his biggest mistakes, he said to God, *"Cast me not away from thy presence; and take not thy holy spirit from me,"* (Psalm 51:11). In my early days, I had people say, *"David you made a lot of mistakes, how is God still elevating you?"* I said, *"I have the covenant of the sure mercies of David!"* When God makes this covenant, He will chasten and correct you when you are wrong and make mistakes, but He will never move you from the position He gave you and no man can either!

Becoming Eternal Kings

Saul's disobedience prevented God from establishing his throne forever. *"... **for now would the LORD have established thy kingdom upon Israel for ever. But now thy kingdom shall not continue:** the LORD hath sought him a man after his own heart,"* (1 Samuel 13:13-14). God replaced Saul with David, and David's throne was established forever because he had the right heart.

*"And thine house and thy kingdom shall be established for ever before thee: **thy throne shall be established for ever,"*** (2 Samuel 7:16).

The covenant of sure mercies is so powerful, preserves your kingship and throne forever. David is not the only person that God made an eternal King, Jesus also promised the twelve apostles that they would have eternal thrones because of their faithfulness in leaving everything and following Him.

*"**And I appoint unto you a kingdom,** as my Father hath appointed unto me; That ye may eat and drink at my table in my kingdom, and sit on thrones judging the twelve tribes of Israel,"* (Luke 22:29-30).

The apostles received eternal kingship in the first three years of their walk with the Lord. Early in my walk, when I was in my early twenties, the Lord took me to heaven to see the position and throne He had for me in the next world. There are people living on earth right now, who are also sitting on thrones in heaven, because of their faithfulness to the Lord. He promises to give you a throne, not just here and now, but for all eternity.

*"Incline your ear, and come unto me: hear, and your soul shall live; and **I will make an everlasting covenant with you, even the sure mercies of David,**"* (Isaiah 55:3).

Through the Blood of Jesus, you have been grafted into the everlasting covenant of sure mercies, and you can have so much more, because God is saying, *"When you get up and meet me in the morning, I will keep making new mercies for you."*

CHAPTER 6
God Awakens You in the Morning

CHAPTER 6
God Awakens You in the Morning

God Awakens for You in the Morning Visitation

"If thy children have sinned against him, and he have cast them away for their transgression; ***If thou wouldest seek unto God betimes,*** *and make thy supplication to the Almighty; If thou wert pure and upright;* ***surely now he would awake for thee,*** *and make the habitation of thy righteousness prosperous,"* (Job 8:4-6).

When you get up early in the morning God awakes for you. The word "betimes" simply means to rise early in the morning or to be up early before dawn. Bildad was basically telling Job, *"If your children have sinned or done something wrong against God all you need to do to reverse the situation, is wake up early in the morning and pray. If you do this God will awake for you. You will get God's attention and He will help you."*

Bildad was giving Job the strategy to turn things around. Job was constantly praying and interceding for his children because they were always doing something wrong. Job's friend was telling him that if he met God in the morning, He would awake for him. "Awake" in Hebrew means to open the eyes, to awake, to lift, raise or stir up oneself. When you wake someone, you get their attention. ***"Awake, why sleepest thou, O Lord? arise,*** *cast us not off for ever,"* (Psalm 44:23). When you seek God early in the morning, He rises and restores you, and deals with people who are fighting you. *"Arise, O LORD, in thine anger, lift up thyself because of the rage of mine enemies: and* ***awake for me to the judgment that***

THE WINGS OF THE MORNING

thou hast commanded," (Psalm 7:6). God awakened when He was angry with the people of Israel, and He cast them out of the land because they forsook Him.

> ***"Then the Lord awaked as one out of sleep, and like a mighty man that shouteth by reason of wine.*** *And he smote his enemies in the hinder parts: he put them to a perpetual reproach,"* (Psalm 78:66).

If you need God to do something, the revelation is to wake up early in the morning and make your supplication to Him. King David understood this mystery and when He was in trouble he prayed, *"Awake, why sleepest thou, O Lord? arise, cast us not off for ever.* ***Wherefore hidest thou thy face, and forgettest our affliction and our oppression?*** *For our soul is bowed down to the dust: our belly cleaveth unto the earth. Arise for our help, and redeem us for thy mercies' sake,"* (Psalm 44:23-26). This proves how critical the face to face move is to our existence. We know that God does not sleep or slumber (Psalm 121:4).

When the Bible talks about God sleeping, it means He is hiding His face from you, He has cast you off, He is turning His back to you and in a sense, He is forgetting you because your relationship with Him is broken. When you offend God and do not repent, His presence lifts off you and He goes back to His place. Believe me, when He turns His face away from you, you are in serious trouble. *"... **thou didst hide thy face, and I was troubled,**"* (Psalm 30:7). However, if you rise to meet Him when He visits the earth in the fourth watch, He will awake for you, turn His face back to you, and the broken relationship will be restored!

> *"I will go and return to my place, till they acknowledge their offence,* ***and seek my face: in their affliction they will seek me early (at dawn)"***
> (Hosea 5:15).

Do you see this? When you experience troublesome times in your relationship with the Lord, God tells you to acknowledge your offense and seek His face early. The word early is *shăchar* in Hebrew and means early in the morning or to dawn. When you seek God early,

God Awakens You in the Morning

He promises to heal and mend the broken relationship, and causes you to live in His sight or His face again (Hosea 6:1-2).

Even if you or the people you are praying for are wrong, when you rise up early, God will awake for you and you will have His attention and He will turn things around. However, this promise is conditioned upon you waking up early. *"If thou wouldest seek God betimes,"* (Job 8:5). The word "if" gives you and I a choice. You can turn everything, that is wrong in your life, around right now if you get up early and meet God on His time. You will get more done because His time is more potent.

Coming Before the Lord at Other Times of the Day

You can expect God to meet you when you come into His presence at any time with singing, praise, and worship. *"Thou meetest him that rejoiceth and worketh righteousness ..."* (Isaiah 64:5). God promises to meet the person who rejoices and works righteousness because His address is Praise. *"But thou art holy, O thou that inhabitest the praises of Israel,"* (Psalm 22:3).

"Serve the LORD with gladness: come before his presence with singing. Enter into his gates with thanksgiving, and into his courts with praise..." (Psalm 100:2,4).

God's presence and visitations are not limited to the morning time. Praise puts you in God's presence. That means you can appear before Him with singing, enter His gates at any time with thanksgiving, and enter His courts with praise. You can do this any time of the day but in the morning, you do not have to praise God for Him to come, He's already here! When God is not physically on the earth, praise, singing, and thanksgiving will take you into His presence.

In an evening service there is minimal praise unless you've been in His presence before the service, however, as praises go up God comes down and inhabits the praises of His people. You can boldly approach God's residence and knock on His door and get Him to come out when you start praising Him, but when you seek God early in the morning you make immediate and direct contact with Him (Isaiah 55:6).

There are two appearances or visitations you can expect in your relationship with the Lord. One is when He visits the earth in the morning, the other is when you go to Him. You get more done when you meet Him on His time, not on yours. In a dream in 2007, the Lord gave me the wings of the morning revelation, *"When you get up to meet me early every morning you make more progress, and you move at a faster pace with me to your destiny, or destination in me, than when you pray to me at any other time of the day."* He also said to me, *"David, whenever you get up and pray in the morning you are meeting me at my time. But when you get up and pray in the morning you are meeting me on your time."*

God makes all things beautiful in *His* time! The fourth watch is God's chosen time to visit the earth and to visit you. To get into the realm where all things come together and work out beautifully in your life, start meeting God when He is on earth in the mornings. When He awakes for you, He makes the habitation of your righteousness prosperous. Your life, ministry, family, business, and everything else will turn around and be successful because you met Him in morning prayer and got His attention!

He Wakes You Up Morning by Morning

"The Lord GOD hath given me the tongue of the learned, that I should know how to speak a word in season to him that is weary: **he wakeneth morning by morning, he wakeneth mine ear to hear as the learned,"** (Isaiah 50:4). God gives you a learned ear and tongue when you meet Him each morning when He visits you in the morning. If you depend on God, He will be your alarm clock and meet you every morning when He visits the earth. He will even send an angel to wake you, if you ask, like Zechariah the prophet experienced.

"And the angel that talked with me came again, and waked me, as a man that is wakened out of his sleep," (Zechariah 4:1).

If you start getting up in the morning, God will keep waking you up like a built-in alarm clock, morning by morning! Have you ever experienced waking up early in the morning three days in a row at the exact same time? That was the Lord waking you up morning by morning, and you must understand that Jehovah is on earth saying, *"Come on, get up. I want to spend time with you."*

It is supernatural when you get up at the same time three nights in a row. That has happened to me several times, when I would wake up suddenly and the clock says 3:33 a.m., then the next night and the night after that, the same exact thing would happen, because God wanted to spend time with me.

There were seasons when I missed the morning time visitation and God quit waking me at that time. However, He did appear to correct me and instruct me to get up and meet Him and He would catch me up with my destiny. Even though He was displeased and stopped waking me up, through His love and correction He showed me how to turn things around by meeting Him on His time. His love truly never fails.

The Significance of God Waking You Up

It is supernatural when God wakes you up at the same time every night, it is Him initiating fourth watch prayer with you. "***Arise, shine; for thy light is come***, *and the glory of the LORD is risen upon thee*" (Isaiah 60:1). It is a call to prayer! There are many who miss the blessings and new mercies that God brings in the morning time visitation because they sleep through it. Peter, James, and John missed grand revelation when they slumbered through most of Moses and Elijah's glorious visit to Jesus on the Mount of Transfiguration.

"And, behold, there talked with him two men, which were Moses and Elias: Who appeared in glory, and spake of his decease which he should accomplish at Jerusalem. ***But Peter and they that were with him were heavy with sleep: and when they were awake,*** *they saw his glory, and the two men that stood with him,"* (Luke 9:30-32).

Jesus took them up the mountain so they could have the inheritance of the saints, but they slept through most of the visitation.

THE WINGS OF THE MORNING

The apostles walked in great kingdom and dominion power because they received it from Jesus, but they never split the seas or called fire down from heaven, like Moses and Elijah did. They could have had that and more, but they missed a great moment, because they *"were heavy with sleep."*

They also slept when Jesus told them to pray in the garden of Gethsemane. ***"And he cometh unto the disciples, and findeth them asleep,** and saith unto Peter, What, could ye not watch with me one hour? Watch and pray, that ye enter not into temptation: the spirit indeed is willing, but the flesh is weak ... And **he came and found them asleep again: for their eyes were heavy,"*** (Matthew 26:40-41,43). Peter, James, and John could not stay awake because "their eyes were heavy," and we know Peter fell into temptation and denied Jesus three times.

Like these three apostles, many believers miss their visitations, simply because they cannot not wake up. However, once you start making the effort to meet the Lord at 3 a.m., consecutively for several nights, you will enter a realm where God wakes you up. *"Let us labour therefore to enter into that rest ... "* (Hebrews 4:11).

"Come unto me, all ye that labour and are heavy laden, and I will give you rest," (Matthew 11:28).

Labor precedes rest! You may struggle and labor at first, but soon after, you will enter the rest of the morning time visitation because the Lord will take away the struggle of waking up. When you are supposed to get up, you will wake up, refreshed, rejuvenated, and ready to pray! Once you get into the rhythm of heaven, God will come, stand by you, and call you like He called Samuel. That way you never ever miss the blessings and the new mercies He has for you in the morning time visitation prayer.

CHAPTER 7
Your Latter End Greatly Increases

CHAPTER 7
Your Latter End Greatly Increases

Fourth Watch Prayer Increases You

"If thou wouldest seek unto God betimes [early], and make thy supplication to the Almighty; **If thou wert pure and upright;** *surely now he would awake for thee, and make the habitation of thy righteousness prosperous.* **Though thy beginning was small, yet thy latter end should greatly increase.."**
(Job 8:5-7).

If you have been praying for God to increase you, combine morning prayer with holiness and righteousness, and He will! The scripture talks about being pure and upright, in addition to making your supplication and prayer, to God "betimes [early]" or at dawn. I have met a lot of Pentecostals who have said, *"God, I have been living pure and upright. I have been living a holy life, why haven't you done this and that for me?"* I asked the Lord why wonderful believers keep asking these questions, and He said, *"They put in their requests at the wrong time."*

"If thou wouldest seek unto God betimes [early] ..." (Job 8:5) God expects you to make your supplication, which is your complaint, requests, and desires known to Him when He is on earth visiting man! When you do, He will awake for you and give you His attention. Mind you, God can answer you at other times of the day, but when you meet Him on His time, He honors you because you honor what He honors!

God has an expected end for you and that end is supposed to be much greater than your beginning. *"Better is the end of a thing than the*

THE WINGS OF THE MORNING

beginning thereof..." (Ecclesiastes 7:8). God starts you off small and then greatly increases you in the end.

I have observed many powerful ministers and preachers that seem to fade the longer they do ministry, but that is not God's way. When you cooperate with God and meet Him early in the morning, you go from glory to glory and your light will burn brighter and brighter until full day! God has a great celebration planned for your end.

David did early morning prayer, and his end was greatly increased! He started out as a shepherd boy in the wilderness, taking care of the sheep, and singing and worshiping God. In fact, his brother rebuked him when he came to see the battle with the Philistines. *"Why camest thou down hither? and with whom hast thou left those few sheep in the wilderness?"* (1 Samuel 17:28). David only had a few sheep in the wilderness when Samuel anointed him to be king, after David killed Goliath, he ran from Saul, and a few men surrounded him during that time when he was a fugitive.

"And every one that was in distress, and every one that was in debt, and every one that was discontented,** gathered themselves unto him; and he became a captain over them: **and there were with him about four hundred men," (1 Samuel 22:2).

David was anointed to be king over millions of Israelites, but God started him off with only 400 men. He faithfully led these men from place to place until Saul died. He returned to Judah, by this time his men increased to 600. *"Awake up, my glory; awake, psaltery and harp: I myself will awake early,"* (Psalm 57:8). David got up early in the morning and sang to the Lord until daybreak and it caused him to continually increase.

"For at that time day by day there came to David to help him, until it was a great host, like the host of God," (1 Chronicles 12:22).

After David was crowned king over Judah, thousands and tens of thousands of powerful warriors joined his army, and it grew to over three hundred thousand men! David kept increasing and increasing for seven years and during that time the house of Saul grew weaker and weaker.

> *"Now there was long war between the house of Saul and the house of David: **but David waxed stronger and stronger,** and the house of Saul waxed weaker and weaker,"* (2 Samuel 3:1).

If you keep doing fourth watch prayer, year by year, you will increase while your enemies grow weaker and weaker. David kept getting bigger and bigger because he met God in morning time visitation prayer! *"My voice shalt thou hear in the morning, O LORD; **in the morning will I direct my prayer unto thee, and will look up,**"* (Psalm 5:3). David was still a shepherd when the prophet Samuel came to Bethlehem to anoint him to be king over Israel. After that, he became a champion and general in Saul's army, and years later he was anointed king over the tribe of Judah.

David Increases Greatly

David increased again, seven years later, when he was anointed the third time as king over the nation of Israel (2 Samuel 5:1-3). This happened twenty years after Samuel first anointed him. David was increasing because the Lord was with him, and when he hit the twentyyear mark, God came in a greater way, as the LORD God of Hosts. You can learn more and gain understanding about the 20-year process in my book titled, *God's Divine Timing Vs. Premature Exposure.*

> *"And David went on, and grew great, and the LORD God of hosts was with him,"* (2 Samuel 5:10).

In my earlier days, when I was in ministry for about 18 years, I had an angelic visitation about how it takes God 18 to 20 years to develop any major leader or general before He promotes them to the forefront, nationally and internationally. The angel told me in my 18th year that I had two more years more to go, then he showed me that when David completed 20 years, the Lord of Hosts began manifesting in his life, and when he truly became great! The angel encouraged me and revealed that when I completed my 20 year process God would come into my life, as the Lord God of Hosts, and when I would become great in America and in many nations around the world!

When David was 37 years old and completed his 20-year process God made him greater. He conquered the Philistines and subdued many of the nations around Israel, brought the ark into Jerusalem, and his name became great all over the world. However, that was not the end for David, God made him an eternal king and established his throne and kingdom forever! *"And David my servant shall be king over them; and they all shall have one shepherd: they shall also walk in my judgments, and observe my statutes, and do them"* (Ezekiel 37:24). Not only is David an eternal King in the next world, he will have a seat of authority on earth during the millennial reign of Christ. His greatness has not ended, it is still increasing!

"O God, thou art my God; early will I seek thee..." (Psalm 63:1-2). I keep because I seek and meet God when He is on earth. When my enemies see the constant persecution and social media attacks against my reputation, they think my destiny will be destroyed, as my enemies did 20 years ago. Satan has intensified the attacks on my ministry, and for many years, my enemies have thought I could never recover, but the Lord God of Hosts is with me and I keep becoming greater and increasing continually.

"But the more they afflicted them, the more they multiplied and grew,"
(Exodus 1:12).

I keep increasing because I know the things that belong to my peace in the morning time visitation. When you wake up early to pray until the breaking of day, God will visit you and cause your latter end to greatly increase. Instead of fading out, becoming tired and worn out, and your reputation, integrity, and legacy in tatters, God wants you to end with a major celebration!

CHAPTER 8
The Ear and Tongue of the Learned

CHAPTER 8
The Ear and Tongue of the Learned

God Gives You the Ear of the Learned in the Morning

"... he wakeneth mine ear to hear as the learned," (Isaiah 50:4).

When God wakes you in the morning, <u>He gives you the ear of the learned</u>, which is needed before you receive the tongue of the learned. The <u>tongue of the learned is given once you hear on the learned level</u>. One blessing of morning time visitations is that God allows you to hear on a frequency that is comparable to people who have studied for years. He will speak to you on such a high revelatory level, that even elders and fathers will be astonished at what you say.

A lot of the fathers around the world ask me, *"David where did you get this type of teaching from? We know you didn't go to any theological school. We've seen theologians sit at your feet and learn from you and they tell us how astonished they are at your doctrine and your wisdom in the word of God."* This happens when you wake up in the morning to pray, seek, and be with the Lord until the breaking of day.

"I have more understanding than all my teachers: *for thy testimonies are my meditation,"* (Psalm 119:99).

David had more understanding than his teachers because he understood morning time visitation prayer. He said, *"O God, thou art my*

God; early will I seek thee ..." (Psalm 63:1). David frequently fellowshipped with the Lord early in the morning, he had the ear of the learned, and walked in great wisdom and revelation beyond that which can be learned in any natural school.

When I got this understanding, many churches and ministries from around the world, wanted to hear me speak because they were hungry and wanted to hear what God has revealed to me. That happened because I started getting up early to meet God after He gave me a series of visitations, wisdom, and revelations about morning time visitation prayer that the nations wanted to hear. The Lord opened the nation of South Korea to me. He put a word in my mouth for that nation when I mastered the morning time and God gave me the ear and tongue of the learned. When you wake up in the morning your hearing changes and people will be shocked at the level of revelation you speak on.

The Learned Ear Closes at Dawn

Whenever God awakens your ear in the morning, it only stays open until the breaking of day. Therefore, whenever God wakes you up early and starts giving you revelations and unspeakable wisdom, you need to write it down before the portal closes. Your spiritual ear is awakened and opened in the morning. Elisha once asked God to open the spiritual eyes of his servant (2 Kings 6:17). In the same way that spiritual eyes can be opened, spiritual ears can be awakened.

I cannot begin to tell you how many words from God that I have missed because I did not write down what He was saying to me. I'm sure many of you reading this book have also experienced times when you heard amazing revelations from God, but when the sun came up and you tried to remember what you heard, and you could not because the ear closed at dawn! When you don't write down what God is saying, the revelation escapes you. *"... he wakeneth morning by morning, he wakeneth mine ear to hear as the learned,"* (Isaiah 50:4). This has also happened to me when God spoke to me in dreams early in the morning, I did not write them down, and I forgot the whole dream.

The Ear and Tongue of the Learned

"He shall fly away as a dream, and shall not be found: yea, he shall be chased away as a vision of the night," (Job 20:8).

When Jehovah comes on earth every morning, He wakens your spiritual ear to hear unmistakable revelations from Him during your fellowship with Him that morning, in a dream, or even when you are studying the Word in the morning. If you do not write down what God tells you the supernatural words vaporize, and the dreams flee away when the morning time visitation is over.

When the children of Israel asked for food God sent them manna at the break of day, *"... **and in the morning the dew lay round about the host.** And when the dew that lay was gone up, behold, upon the face of the wilderness there lay a small round thing, as small as the hoar frost on the ground,"* (Exodus 16:13-14). Proving again that God visits the earth in the morning. Bread also symbolizes the Word of God and what happened to the manna when the sun came up?

*"And they gathered it every morning (dawn), every man according to his eating: **and when the sun waxed hot, it melted,**"* (Exodus 16:21).

This is a parable explains what happens, when you do not capture what God releases while the learned ear is open, before the sun rises and it closes. Like the manna melted, the revelation escapes you.

When Jacob and the angel wrestled all night, Jacob got a blessing, a name change, and become a prince, because he held on to the angel and would not let him go until he blessed him. You must have the tenacity in the spirit to hold on to what God reveals to you, and you do that by writing down what the Lord reveals to you, because once the sun rises, the learned ear closes up.

If you do not capture that moment by writing down what you receive with the learned ear then when the Lord leaves the earth at daybreak together with all the angels that came with Him in that visitation, then that revelation leaves too. There are occasions when God seals instructions in your ear. ***"Then he openeth the ears of men, and*** *sealeth their instruction,"* (Job 33:16). When He does, the revelation is established in your spirit, later in the day it will suddenly come to you. However, for the most part, when God opens your ear in the morning, He expects you to capture that moment by writing down the vision or revelation He gives you so you do not lose it at daybreak, when He leaves.

Operating in the Learned Realm
The Lord Disciples You in the Morning Visitation

A disciple has the potential to become like the master. *"The disciple is not above his master: but every one that is perfect shall be as his master"* (Luke 6:40). In my own ministry, most of the people I teach and disciple, become spiritual giants because they are fed giant food. They are served revelation at a giant level because of the realm I operate in. That is great, but do you realize that it is far greater for the Lord to personally take you on as His own disciple and teach you? It is okay for a great man of God to teach you and your ears open to learn from him, but it is an entirely different thing for God Almighty to teach you. When He visits the earth every morning, that is what He is doing. If you hear what He has to say, you will function on a whole different level.

*"... I thank thee, O Father, Lord of heaven and earth, because **thou hast hid these things from the wise and prudent, and hast revealed them unto babes.** Even so, Father: for so it seemed good in thy sight,"* (Matthew 11:25-26).

The Father revealed things to Jesus' disciples that He would not even share with the "wise and prudent." The apostles were babies in their development, and they were receiving revelations that wise and prudent people should have been receiving, because they were receiving blessings of morning time visitation and becoming learned people! *"The Lord GOD hath given me the tongue of the learned ... he wakeneth mine ear to hear as the learned,"* (Isaiah 50:4). "Learned" in the Hebrew means to be instructed, to be a disciple, to be taught, learned. When God wakens you morning by morning and gives you the ear and tongue of the learned He is discipling you!

The Ear and Tongue of the Learned

A person on my staff had a powerful dream where he heard a voice saying to him, *"The Maker of the Mornings shall be your teacher."* God Himself becomes your teacher in the fourth watch. *"The Lord GOD hath given me the tongue of the learned, that I should know how to speak a word in season to him that is weary:* **he wakeneth morning by morning, he wakeneth mine ear to hear as the learned,** *"* (Isaiah 50:4). God becomes your teacher when He visits you in the fourth watch.

Most believers know that Jesus and the Holy Spirit are also teachers, but did you know that the Father is a teacher? How would you like to be taught by Jehovah God when He visits the earth? *"It is written in the prophets,* **And they shall be all taught of God.** *Every man therefore that hath* **heard, and hath learned of the Father, cometh unto me,** *"* (John 6:45). All shall be taught of God when they do the morning time visitation prayer.

You call tell the rank and level of a prophet by the words they speak. God will not raise up what I call a jackleg or backyard prophet, who is slacking, and put them on the national scene. Samuel, for example, was established by God to be a national prophet from his early days. *"And all Israel from Dan even to Beersheba knew that Samuel was established to be a prophet of the LORD,"* (1 Samuel 3:20). All Israel recognized that Samuel was going to have a national ministry because he had a national word. *"And ere the lamp of God went out in the temple of the LORD, where the ark of God was, and Samuel was laid down to sleep,"* (1 Samuel 3:3). Samuel was in the presence of the Lord continually, which cannot be said of many prophets and preachers.

The lamps were relit every morning, therefore God appeared to him right before sunrise. *"And Aaron shall burn thereon sweet incense* **every morning: when he dresseth the lamps,** *"* (Exodus 30:7). The word for morning means dawn or the break of day (Exodus 27:20-21; 30:7-8). God's pattern of causing his prophets to wake up early every morning with a word is confirmed here. Samuel became a national prophet because he diligently did the morning time visitation.

117

THE WINGS OF THE MORNING

To be a national prophet or to operate at a high level in ministry you need the learned ear which only opens during the morning time visitation prayer. God will not put you on the national scene if you are slothful. You must be diligent in waking up to meet God when He comes on the earth. God cannot make you a national prophet if you do not wake up early enough to get a word for the nation.

If you do not study long enough to be learned in the realm you are operating, you cannot be approved or promoted to the next stage. *"Study to shew thyself approved unto God, a workman that needeth not to be ashamed, rightly dividing the word of truth,"* (2 Timothy 2:15). "Study" means to use speed, to be prompt, and to be diligent. In the Old Testament, when the word diligent is used, oftentimes it means rising early in the morning to do your tasks, and it is why God gives you the ear of the learned early in the morning when you rise up!

When you are "approved unto God," you will rightly divide His Word and be exalted by God to reach higher dimensions in Him and when you capture or keep what He tells you in the morning you become wise beyond your years. God allows you to hear and understand things that normally would not learn for another ten years. *"I understand more than the ancients, **because I keep thy precepts,**"* (Psalm 119:100).

Speaking with a Learned Tongue

***"The Lord GOD hath given me the tongue of the learned, that I should know how to speak a word in season to him that is weary:** he wakeneth morning by morning, he wakeneth mine ear to hear as the learned,"* (Isaiah 50:4).

Another blessing of the morning time visitation is the tongue of the learned. You cannot have the tongue of the learned if you do not have the ear of the learned because you cannot speak what you are not hearing. *"I can of mine own self do nothing: as I hear, I judge…"* (John 5:30). God gives you the tongue of the learned when He wakens your ear in the morning, and you begin to speak on a whole different frequency that can reach more people and have a greater impact.

Hear then speak.

The Ear and Tongue of the Learned

*"I have not sent these prophets, yet they ran: **I have not spoken to them, yet they prophesied,"*** (Jeremiah 23:21).

Too many prophets run off to speak a word when they have not heard from the Lord causing a lot of casualties in the body of Christ. When you have the tongue of the learned you *"speak a word in season to him that is weary,"* if you operate outside of the learned realm you break and crush the spirit of the weary with words spoken presumptuously. When you get up and pray from 3 a.m. until daybreak, God will speak to you in the darkness of the secret place. *"What I tell you in darkness, that speak ye in light: and what ye hear in the ear, that preach ye upon the housetops,"* (Matthew 10:27). When you meet God, at the time He visits the earth, you will be able to speak forth what the ear of the learned hears!

God Makes Me a General

When I started waking up in the morning, my voice gained more authority and God started to elevate me nationally. I can tell you that the sound of my voice was changing, and other things began happening in my ministry, as I was making great progress and catching up to where God wanted me to be in ministry. Then He made me a general.

I was in a season when I was getting up many nights and praying until daybreak, and one night I had a dream. In the dream, I saw four stars on the ground, I heard a voice, but I did not see anyone. Instinctively, I knew it was the voice of the Lord. He said, *"Pick up the stars."* I bent over and picked up the stars, then I heard Him say, *"You are now a four-star general."* As I looked at the four stars in my hands somehow, I knew a fifth one was missing. At the same time, I heard, *"You will get the fifth star when the move of God hits St. Louis as I told you."* Then I woke up.

There are very few five-star generals in America, most are four-star generals. Five-star generals attain that rank only when they lead the army in the act of war. I was amazed and humbled by the promotion in the dream. I knew what generals were from my study of the book, *God's Generals* by Roberts Liardon, but I wanted to understand what a general really was in God's eyes. I was spending morning time prayer with the Lord and wondering about the dream.

Two days later, after morning prayer, a prophetess called me and told me that God gave her a dream about me. In the dream, she saw an old man she knew was from heaven, who may have possibly been one of the 24 elders that sit around God's throne in heaven. She said, *"He was standing in front of you and he looked up to heaven and said, 'I thank You Father, for giving me the honor to do this,'"* and then, *"He put a general cap on your head and said, 'general!'"* Then she asked me if I knew what the dream meant. I was amazed at the divine confirmation. She had no idea that two days earlier God called me a general in a dream. God confirms what He's saying to you when you do this kind of prayer.

When you get up in the morning to meet God, He changes your rank, because you cannot speak to kings if you don't hear a word at that level, and you cannot speak to nations if you are not hearing national words. You get to this realm when you operate in the learned ear and tongue realm.

"I know thy works, that thou hast a name that thou livest, and art dead,"
(Revelation 3:1).

You do not get the learned ear by attending divinity schools and seminaries. They have a reputation of being alive, but they are dead. They empty everything out of the people who attend and put out their fire. If you get your learning from institutions, you better keep your fire by staying connected to the presence of God. The Lord did not place me on the national scene because I got a Ph.D. or THD from a divinity school, I got my rank and placement by getting up early in the morning and meeting the Lord when He visits the earth. The Lord faithfully woke me, morning by morning, and gave me a learned ear and tongue.

CHAPTER 9

What Happens in the Morning

CHAPTER 9
What Happens in the Morning

You Receive a Prophetic Word in the Morning

When you wake up to meet God in the morning, He gives you a prophetic word. Jesus, God's premier prophet, can personally come to you with the answer or He will send another prophet with a word for you. God wakes up His prophets with a word for His people early in the morning, *"Since the day that your fathers came forth out of the land of Egypt unto this day I have even sent unto you all my servants the prophets, **daily rising up early and sending them,**"* (Jeremiah 7:25).

*"**And the LORD hath sent unto you all his servants the prophets, rising early and sending them;** but ye have not hearkened, nor inclined your ear to hear,"* (Jeremiah 25:4).

*"**Because they have not hearkened to my words,** saith the LORD, which I sent unto them by my servants **the prophets, rising up early and sending them;** but ye would not hear, saith the LORD,"* (Jeremiah 29:19).

These scriptures about prophets rising early refers to how God wakes His prophets early in the morning with a word for His people. God does not send His prophets at noon or in the evening, He sends them early in the morning when He is visiting the earth. God may not send a prophetic word to you every day that you meet Him in morning prayer, but He will when you are in a season of morning prayer. Most people receive dreams from God early in the morning. He will speak directly to you but not tell you everything. He uses other people to confirm what He's saying and to tell you things you cannot quite hear.

It is true that if you do not get up in the morning you become a weak prophet or prophetess, because it is God's pattern. Don't get me wrong, God can send prophets at other times of the day, but He has a schedule for sending His prophets out early in the morning, when He is on earth, with a word for His people. Prophets need to be early risers to hear what He wants them to speak.

Getting up early gives you an accurate prophetic word and increases the level your word will be spoken. I have seen prophets operating in storefront churches who are accurate, but their ministries are not at a level where more are reached, because their word is on a lower frequency. Only by meeting God on His time can He trust you with a greater frequency and deeper dimension in ministry and elevate you to a national platform.

God requires prophets to get up early in the morning so they can hear His Word with a learned ear and speak with a learned tongue. This makes the difference between a storefront prophet and a national prophet, and a national prophet and an international prophet. Local prophets get local words, national and international prophets speak on a much higher level, because they pay the price to wake up early in the morning to meet God! If you do not get up to meet Him, He cannot awaken your ear to hear things on a higher level, so you can speak to a larger group of people. I have seen prophets stay at the same level for years because their hearing is at the same level.

"The Lord GOD hath given me the tongue of the learned, that I should know how to speak a word in season to him that is weary: *he wakeneth morning by morning, he wakeneth mine ear to hear as the learned"*
(Isaiah 50:4).

What Happens in the Morning

When prophets get around me their ministries go to another level, because I teach them the principle of rising early in the morning. The prophetic ministry of Moses was unprecedented, because God woke him up early in the morning and sent him to Pharaoh.

God's Early Morning Pattern with His Prophets

*"And the LORD God of their fathers **sent to them by his messengers, rising up betimes, and sending;** because he had compassion on his people, and on his dwelling place: But they mocked the messengers of God, and despised his words, and misused his prophets, until the wrath of the LORD arose against his people, till there was no remedy,"* (2 Chronicles 36:15-16).

God's pattern with His prophets has never changed. All prophets who work with God, have morning ministries. *"To hearken to the words of my servants the prophets, whom I sent unto you, **both rising up early, and sending them,** but ye have not hearkened"* (Jeremiah 26:5). God sent Moses with a word for Pharaoh because it is a significant time in a prophet's ministry.

*"**And the LORD said unto Moses, Rise up early in the morning, and stand before Pharaoh;** lo, he cometh forth to the water; and say unto him, Thus saith the LORD, Let my people go, that they may serve me,"* (Exodus 8:20).

*"And the LORD said unto **Moses, Rise up early in the morning, and stand before Pharaoh,** and say unto him, Thus saith the LORD God of the Hebrews, Let my people go, that they may serve me,"* (Exodus 9:13).

God repeatedly told Moses to rise *"early in the morning"* to meet Pharaoh with the prophetic word. He wakens your ear morning by morning and gives you the tongue of the learned so you can give a word to His people in season.

I received a major message for South Korea during a morning visitation. When Jesus appeared before me, He spoke about the reunification of South and North Korea and how it would happen in the span of five years. I received an invitation to South Korea around the same time I received this word 2013. When I arrived, I gave them the word and five years later, in 2018, the word came to pass exactly as Jesus said it would! When you get up in the morning God will give you direction that will change nations!

God Sends Prophets with Answers in the Morning

Through the years, I have noticed that whenever I get up early in the morning to pray, I get a prophetic word. Many times prophets who have not called in more than a year, will call or text and say, *"God told me to tell you this"* or *"God woke me up with a dream about you and told me to tell you this."* When this happens, it is exactly what I needed to hear concerning what I was dealing with in prayer. God will put you on somebody's heart even if they are not a prophet and use them in the prophetic realm to give you a word when you do fourth watch prayer. One morning in 2013, when I was up praying at 3 a.m. in a hotel in South Korea, I got a call from someone who said, *"I had a dream about you this morning. God showed me that He's going to give you answers. These answers are coming to you."* While I was on my knees, meeting God that morning, He gave answers to my prayers in another person's dream! God will do that for you too because morning time prayer accelerates answers to prayers. *"... one day is with the Lord as a thousand years, and a thousand years as one day,"* (2 Peter 3:8). When God is on the earth with you in the morning, and depending on your level of maturity with Him, in just one day you can accomplish what it would take you one thousand years to do!

When you pray in the evening and during the day, many times you wait for weeks and months to get answers. However, in morning prayer, God is on earth and He sends prophets or prophetic words to accelerate answers to your prayer. This is what I was praying about that morning in South Korea. *"Lord, you sent an angel to tell me in a dream years ago that you were calling me to be the healing shepherd over America and to take over the healing platform that you gave Pastor Benny to pray for the sick.*

What Happens in the Morning

You told me in this dream that you were going to send Benny overseas but that you did not want to leave America without a healing shepherd."

In this dream, an angel told me that my healing ministry will be many times bigger than that of Benny because the amount of sick people was greater than in Benny's days. The angel said, *"God said, 'I'm going to move Benny Hinn overseas because I have work for him to do there and I am leaving America open for you to minister to the people."* Not long after I had this dream, and without saying anything to Pastor Benny, he told the people who attended one of his crusades, *"God told me I have to move the miracle crusades out of America and go overseas."* Some of the fathers I previously shared the dream with were there, and said, *"What you saw in the dream has happened!"*

When I was praying about the dream, I was saying, *"What do I do, Lord? I need the right connections to make this happen. I need the right answers. I don't know how to make something that big happen. I don't know what to do. I don't know who to really connect with to pray for the sick on the level that Benny did. Lord, you need to help me."* Right when the sun came up that morning, my phone rang, it was a great leader with a massive ministry in California who packs out arenas in America. He said, *"David, we are getting ready to do all the arenas in America again. God told me to call you this morning. He wants you to lead this. Not only face to face but also to pray for the masses in America."* God was answering me because I got up early and prayed from 3 a.m. until the breaking of day!

When you get up early to pray, God accelerates your destiny, gives you answers to what you are praying for, and sends a prophetic word that accelerates your destiny. Has God promised to do certain things for you in dreams and visions? If you do morning prayer, God will answer you. Since 2012, He established me as the healing shepherd to America, and every year it gets bigger and bigger. God has performed what He promised me many years ago and He will do the same for you!

God Changes Your Name in the Morning
Your Character and Identity Changes in the Morning

"Thy name shall be called no more Jacob, but Israel..." (Genesis 32:28).

Morning prayer causes God to change your name, because a name identifies you and embodies your nature, character, and destiny. Gabriel said to Joseph, *"And she (Mary) shall bring forth a son, and **thou shalt call his name JESUS: for he shall save his people from their sins,***" (Matthew 1:21). "Jesus" means salvation and that is why God sent Him to save the world! Moses is another prophetic name, *"And she called his name Moses: and she said, **Because I drew him out of the water,***" (Exodus 2:10). The name Moses means drawn out of water and why he turned the waters of Egypt into blood, brought frogs out of the River Nile, split and closed the Red Sea, and brought water out of a rock. His name prophetically spoke about his destiny. To be named wrong can be disastrous to your life. When Jacob asked for a blessing, the angel asked him what his name was, because if he was going to bless him, his name had to be changed.

God was with Jacob even though he had an evil character. In Hebrew, Jacob's name means, a heel catcher, a supplanter, someone who deceives, and by name and experience Jacob lived up to the meaning of his name. He deceived Esau out of his birthright, and years later deceived his father Isaac into giving him the blessing he intended to give Esau. For more than 90 years Jacob was a heel catcher, supplanter, and a deceiver. However, in just one morning time visitation, God changed his name and his character! Morning time visitation changes *you*. This is the account in scripture, *"And Jacob was left alone; and there wrestled a man with him until the breaking of the day. And when he saw that he prevailed not against him, he touched the hollow of his thigh; and the hollow of Jacob's thigh was out of joint, as he wrestled with him. **And he said, Let me go, for the day breaketh.** And he said, I will not let thee go, except thou bless me. And he said unto him, What is thy name? And he said, Jacob. And he said, **Thy name shall be called no more Jacob, but Israel:** for as a prince hast thou power with God and with men, and hast prevailed,"* (Genesis 32:24-28).

Jacob was alone when he had this experience. When you are in prayer, you need an "alone" place. Jesus also loved to pray alone. *"And when he had sent the multitudes away, **he went up into a mountain apart to pray: and when the evening was come, he was there alone,"*** (Matthew 14:23).

Jesus Renames His Disciples at Daybreak

Naming also denotes your glory, fame, and personality. God calls each star by name because they differ from the other in glory (Psalm 147:4; Corinthians 15:41). Renaming is a divine way for God to change your character, identity, and nature so you can fulfill a certain assignment and destiny in life, like He did with Jacob as soon as he was renamed. After that morning time visitation, he was humble and broken, and this change in his character opened the door for the two brothers to reconcile. God also changes your name when He wants to inaugurate you into your true destiny.

*"Neither shall thy name any more be called Abram, but thy name shall be **Abraham;** for a father of many nations have I made thee,"* (Genesis 17:5).

For God to make Abram a father of many nations, He had to change his name to Abraham! Once the name was changed, Abraham was established as a patriarchal father of many nations and came into the office of a divine emperor and birther of kings! *"And I will make thee exceeding fruitful, and I will make nations of thee, and kings shall come out of thee,"* (Genesis 17:6). The new name transformed his procreative abilities, his body was dead, but right after he received his new name, Abraham and Sarah had a son! There are examples of how God-given names pinpointed the life and destiny of people like Seth, the sons of Jacob, Naboth, Jabez, and John. Throughout the Old Testament, God used the power of naming, to prophesy the destiny of His people. He even gave prophetic messages to Israel through the names He commanded His prophets to give their children (Isaiah 8:3; Hosea 1:4,6,9).

THE WINGS OF THE MORNING

In the New Testament, Jesus followed the same practice in His Father's business. *"Verily, verily, I say unto you,* **The Son can do nothing of himself, but what he seeth the Father do:** *for what things soever he doeth, these also doeth the Son likewise,"* (John 5:19). Jesus gave new names and titles to His apostles after He prayed all through the night, until the breaking of day.

"And it came to pass in those days, that he went out into a mountain to pray, **and continued all night in prayer to God. And when it was day,** *he called unto him his disciples:* **and of them he chose twelve, whom also he named apostles;** *Simon, (whom he also named Peter,) and Andrew his brother, James and John, Philip and Bartholomew,"* (Luke 6:12-14).

At dawn, Jesus called His twelve disciples "apostles," meaning they were set apart as sent ones, or delegates. For the first time in the Bible, this title was used and the disciples were established as eternal kings, and their names were embedded in the foundations of New Jerusalem! *"And the wall of the city had twelve foundations,* **and in them the names of the twelve apostles of the Lamb,"** (Revelation 21:14). Peter, James, and John, Jesus' premier disciples, were given special names.

"...And when Jesus beheld him, he said, **Thou art Simon the son of Jona: thou shalt be called Cephas,** *which is by interpretation, A stone,"*
(John 1:42).

"And Simon he surnamed Peter; *And James the son of Zebedee, and John the brother of James; and* **he surnamed them Boanerges,** *which is, The sons of thunder,"* (Mark 3:16-17).

Jesus renamed Simon as Peter or Cephas, He knew that Simon was going to go through certain trials that Satan designed to uproot and destroy him, but when Jesus renamed him, Peter became a rock that could not be removed and solidified Peter in the apostolic ministry. Even though Peter was shaken, he was not uprooted. Jesus surnamed James and John, sons of thunder! Do you see how important names are in the Kingdom of God? Paul's apostolic ministry shifted into high gear when he stopped going by "Saul," his original Jewish name, and started going by "Paul," his Gentile name. The Gentile world was opened to receive his ministry.

God Changes My Middle Name

I hope you are seeing why it is important for God to name you. Many of you are going to get new names in the spirit when the Lord visits you in dreams and visions during the fourth watch. For some, He will change your name completely. For example, David Yonggi Cho, the pastor of the largest church in the world, was visited by the Lord and his names was changed from Paul to David. Shortly after that happened, God started drawing the masses to his ministry. When God renames you, your character, identity, and destiny are transformed.

The Lord changed my name in 2010, when Jesus Christ was revealing more and more of the Father to me. Until that point, my fellowship was mainly with Jesus and the Holy Spirit, I had few interactions with the Father before entering 20 years in ministry. They began in 2006 when Jesus appeared to me and said, *"The time has come for me to deliver you over to the Father. I have been teaching you all this time together with the Holy Spirit, but now the Father is going to be teaching you. I will not stop coming to you but now is the time of the Father for you."* I know that this may sound farfetched to many believers, but you must understand that Jehovah wants us to fellowship with all three members of the Godhead.

The Father, Son, and Holy Spirit are three different persons, but because they agree, they are one. *"For there are three that bear record in heaven, the Father, the Word, and the Holy Ghost: and these three are one,"* (1 John 5:7). This is a rebuke to the false "Oneness" doctrine, that tries to lump the Father, Son, and the Holy Spirit into one person. That is not true.

I deal extensively on this subject in my book entitled, *"The God Realm in The Kingdom of God."* Not long after this visitation, I prophesied that the Father was going to appear to me openly, and His first major appearance in the clouds, happened in Spokane, Washington. The Father appeared in a fiery rainbow over the city for a full hour and "National Geographic" captured the notable appearance in their magazine. Jewels fell from heaven during the

THE WINGS OF THE MORNING

phenomenal appearance. Here are pictures of the Spokane appearance and some of the jewels that fell.

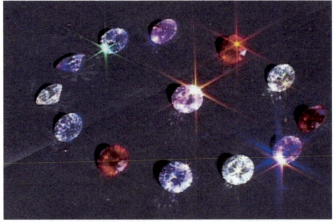

Prophetess Patricia King also saw this happen. I'm sharing the background story of how God changed my name, so you develop the right honor and understanding of what it is for God to change your name and what it about. In 2006, the first notable face to face appearance happened. In 2008, after I had been walking with the Lord for 18 years, He sent an angel to give me a very critical revelation about spiritual maturity and sonship that completely changed my life. The angel said, *"It takes God 18 to 20 years to raise up a true apostle, prophet, or general on the national scene."* The angel explained that 18 to 20 years is the process of time and training that God requires of leaders to go through, before He gives them national prominence. <u>The angel cautioned me and said that anyone who is promoted prematurely, on a national scale, never makes it unless they go through God's process, because they end up casting their fruit in the field, before its time</u> (Malachi 3:11).

When the angel said, "18 to 20 years," I was excited because at the time of this visitation, I was in my eighteenth year with the Lord. However, the angel said, *"You are not ready yet because Jesus is the only person who ever accomplished this process in 18 years. It takes every other man 20 years because of the fall of Adam. This is your 18th year but you are still not ready. It's going to take an extra two years before the Father will publicly come down on earth and work with you openly in front of America and the world."* That does not mean that the Father cannot start working with you earlier in the process, He does come to train you to work with Him, like He did in 2006. When He openly appeared in Spokane, Washington with me. That visitation was a taste of what was coming when I fully matured.

Jesus also visited me during this season and told me that the key to working with God is meekness. He told me that I developed humility, but not enough meekness to work with the Father. Walking with the Lord in fellowship is different than working with Him. You need humility to walk with God. *"... to walk humbly with thy God?"* (Micah 6:8). However, to have God come on earth and manifest Himself in the sight of all men, takes a well-developed heart of meekness. <u>God worked on earth with Moses because he developed enough meekness</u>. *"Now the man Moses was very meek, above all the men which were upon the face of the earth"* (Numbers 12:3). I listened to Jesus' words and immediately started developing meekness. In 2010, after I passed the test of meekness, the Father came to me in a dream. He was in a pillar of fire as I saw Him descend from Heaven to Earth, and He said, *"David this is your 20th year, I am with you. I am now with you in a special way. Your real ministry to the nation and the world is about to begin."*

This moment in the visitation confirmed what the angel said to me two years earlier. It takes 20 years for us to mature enough to work directly with the Father. My twenty years of training started late in 1989 and was completed in 2010.

At this point in the dream, the Father spoke to me about my middle name. When I was born, my mother named me David E. Taylor, and the "E" was for Edward. However, the Father said to me, *"The 'E' will not be for Edward anymore, your middle name is now Emmanuel, because I am on earth working with you."* This is also when He told me that He raised me up to be His face to face prophet to American and the Nations of the world, like Moses was. To confirm this, God sent a prophet who was following my ministry for many years to give me this prophetic word, *"I had a strange dream about you. All I know is that God changed your name in the dream and your name is Emmanuel."* This was a glorious confirmation because I never told anyone that the Father appeared to me and changed my name, nobody knew but me.

After that confirmation, I legally changed my middle name from Edward to Emmanuel, because it speaks of my destiny, God with us! *"Behold, a virgin shall be with child, and shall bring forth a son, and they shall call **his name Emmanuel, which being interpreted is, God with us"*** (Matthew 1:23). This is not just a spiritual cliché it means God physically comes from heaven to dwell with men. Jesus had that name, because He was God manifested in the flesh, dwelling among men, so mankind can meet with the father. The face to face movement is about God notably coming on earth in the sight of America and the nations of the world. *"And Moses brought forth the people out of the camp to meet with God"* (Exodus 19:17). Like Moses, my assignment is to bring people to meet God, and He changed my middle name to Emmanuel, because I am a face to face prophet like Moses and Jesus! I received this because of fourth watch prayer!

At Dawn You Receive a New Name

God wants to give you a new name (Revelation 2:17). There are areas in your character that have not been changed, because you have missed the morning time visitation, and things in your life and destiny have become stagnate, because you did not know that a name change in the fourth watch belongs to your peace. The next morning you rise up in prayer, ask God to bless you by proclaiming a new name over your life, and He will!

You Come into the Inheritance of the Fathers
You Receive Spiritual Inheritance in the Fourth Watch

"If thou wouldest seek unto God betimes, and make thy supplication to the Almighty; If thou wert pure and upright; surely now he would awake for thee, and make the habitation of thy righteousness prosperous. Though thy beginning was small, yet thy latter end should greatly increase. **For enquire, I pray thee, of the former age, and prepare thyself to the search of their fathers:** *(For we are but of yesterday, and know nothing, because our days upon earth are a shadow:)* **Shall not they teach thee, and tell thee, and utter words out of their heart?"** (Job 8:5-10).

When God awakes for you in the morning time visitation, He brings you into the spiritual inheritance, power, and glory from the fathers of the former age! I had a series of visitations and trips to heaven in which God gave me this epic revelation about the inheritance of the fathers.

During one trip, I met Kathryn Kuhlman, Smith Wigglesworth, and other fathers and generals of faith. After I experienced these trips and visitations, I started walking in incredible power and glory. Like Kathryn Kuhlman, blue lightnings, and strong winds have come from the Father's presence into my miracle crusades, like Smith Wigglesworth, I have seen many people raised from the dead, and I came into the inheritance of the fathers because I met God and prayed during the fourth watch!

I wrote extensively about these revelations and trips to heaven in my book *"Inheritance by Lineage: Finding Your Identity,"* it will bless your life and ministry. God never intended for you to struggle, there is a rich and wealthy inheritance in the fathers, to start your spiritual life with wealth! Jesus told His disciples, *"I sent you to reap that whereon ye bestowed no labour:* ***other men laboured, and ye are entered into their*** *labours,"* (John 4:38). There is a place in God where He allows you to enter the labors of other men, that is, the fathers that came before you.

Walking in the Spiritual Inheritance of the Fathers

You are not supposed to sweat and labor in vain when you have a wealth of spiritual inheritance laid up for you to walk in! When you seek God betimes, He will allow the spirit and power of the fathers, and the riches of His glory come upon your life.

I came into my Mosaic Lineage inheritance when I did the morning time visitation prayer. God the Father appeared to me in 2006 and said, *"I have raised you up to be a face to face prophet in this generation. I have given you what Moses had."* Face to face prophets are not like other prophets that God raises up in every generation, they are a rare breed that God raises up once, every 2,000 years. Moses was the first face to face prophet.

"And there arose not a prophet since in Israel like unto Moses, whom the LORD knew face to face" (Deuteronomy 34:10).

Moses was a prophet that God knew face to face. Two thousand years later, Jesus was raised up to be a face to face prophet like unto Moses. This was prophesied by Moses when he said, *"The LORD thy God will raise up unto thee a Prophet from the midst of thee, of thy brethren, like unto me; unto him ye shall hearken"* (Deuteronomy 18:15). Many of the same things that happened to Moses happened to Jesus. For example, Pharaoh issued an edict to kill all the baby boys at the birth of Moses, Herod issued an edict to kill all the boys in Bethlehem when Jesus was born. Moses turned water into blood, Jesus turned water into wine. Jesus spoke about the connection and lineage between Him and Moses.

"For had ye believed Moses, ye would have believed me: for he wrote of me. But if ye believe not his writings, how shall ye believe my words?" (John 5:46-47).

In other words, Jesus was saying, *"I am the prophet Moses prophesied about. I am a face to face prophet like unto him."* Jesus did not come into it because it was prophesied, or because He was the only begotten Son of God. He paid the price to come into the inheritance of the fathers with morning prayer! Jesus did not just pay the price to come into the Mosaic lineage, He paid to come into all the lineages and inheritances of the fathers that came before Him! *"Think not that I am come to destroy the law, or the prophets: I am not come to destroy, but to fulfil,"* (Matthew 5:17). Jesus did not destroy what the fathers did, He came to fulfill, complete, and perfect them. Because He frequently got up a great while before day and prayed until dawn, He came into the spiritual inheritance of the fathers.

"And beginning at Moses and all the prophets, he expounded unto them in all the scriptures the things concerning himself," (Luke 24:27).

Another 2,000 years have passed, and God has raised me up to be the face to face prophet in this generation like unto Moses. Not long after the Father visited me and told me this, He started appearing in the clouds and multitudes of people were seeing Him in many of the places He sent me, as He did with Moses, and this continues to happen everywhere I go. God told Moses to meet Him early in the morning if he wanted to see His glory, I did that, and now His glory is manifesting all over the world through the Face to Face Movement! Morning time visitation prayer brings you into the ancient power and glory of the fathers! If you get up at betimes and make supplication, your latter end will greatly increase, as you possess what your fathers stored up for you and take it to the next level!

A Blessing is Pronounced on You in the Morning
The Blessing Comes at Daybreak

"Yet a little sleep, a little slumber, a little folding of the hands to sleep: So shall thy poverty come as one that travelleth; and thy want as an armed man," (Proverbs 24:33-34).

You can lose the new mercies that God brings to you in the morning if you do not win the battle against slumber. Whatever blessings you are supposed to receive in the morning can be denied or taken from you if you do not fight off sleep. Just a little sleep and a little slumber can open the door for the thief to break into your house and walk off with everything you have. The wrestle and challenge you face during morning time prayer is fighting off drowsiness and slumber. You must win this fight because *"... drowsiness shall clothe a man with rags,"* (Proverbs 23:21). The spirit of slumber attacks believers when they need to pray, therefore, Jesus commands us to watch and pray!

Put Your Request in at Dawn

"And he said, Let me go, for the day breaketh. And he said, I will not let thee go, except thou bless me," (Genesis 32:26).

Jacob wrestled with the angel all night and got a blessing at daybreak. When I teach this kind of prayer in churches, I usually organize early morning prayer and we meet in the church from 3 a.m. until daybreak. I notice that the moment they see the morning light coming forth the people start leaving. but that is *not* the time to leave or go to sleep, it is the time to put your request in.

Carnal believers find this principle hard to receive, but it is the real point of morning prayer. You must die to the flesh before you receive from God, who is a spirit. You have to be positioned in the right place so your flesh dies, and your spirit receives. You never know the exact time He's coming you just need to be up. Sometimes He comes at 3 a.m. on the dot, He might come at 3:30 a.m., and other times He may come at 4 or 5 a.m. You do not really know, but know this, He *will* come!

God requires you to put your requests in at daybreak because when the fourth watch is over, and the day is breaking, the morning time prayer transitions and you go to God with your requests. He expects you to put in your request after He's done talking to you about everything that is on *His* heart. When He's finished dealing with what He wants to talk about at the breaking of day, it's your turn. He waits on you before He leaves.

Many believers miss this opportunity because they have not been taught what I am sharing now. Jacob wrestled with the angel all night, which represents a battle between the flesh during prayer. When Peter struggled with drowsiness in the garden of Gethsemane, Jesus said, *"... **Simon, sleepest thou?** couldest not thou watch one hour? Watch ye and pray, lest ye enter into temptation. **The spirit truly is ready, but the flesh is weak,"*** (Mark 14:37-38). We can accurately surmise *"the spirit truly is ready, but the flesh is weak"* as the wrestle!

In the prayer wrestle, you must stay awake, prevail, and persevere in prayer until the breaking of day! Jacob wrestled with the angel until daybreak, and when the angel told Jacob he must leave, Jacob refused to let him go and said, *"... I will not let thee go, except thou bless me."* This is what you must understand, when the day is breaking it is not the time to let go or stop praying, it is time to ask for a blessing by making your requests known to the Lord!

"And he said unto him, What is thy name? And he said, Jacob,"
(Genesis 32:27).

Daybreak is the time God listens to your requests and deals with what is on your heart! This revelation will change your life if you receive it. At daybreak, the angel said, *"Okay Jacob, I'm done with you. I need to go."* Jacob argued, *"Oh no, this is my time. You must bless me before I let you go."* Too many people get up from prayer too early. Learn to prevail in prayer until daybreak and when as daylight comes, put your requests in, and God will grant you with new mercies!

Joy Comes in the Morning
The Bucket of Joy

"Therefore with joy shall ye draw water out of the wells of salvation,"
(Isaiah 12:3).

Joy is another thing that belongs to your peace when you meet God in the fourth watch. When does joy come? It comes in the morning! If you suffer from depression, get up and pray in the morning, because joy comes in the morning. When you get up to pray in the morning God will give you beauty for ashes, the oil of joy for mourning, and a garment of praise for the spirit of heaviness (Isaiah 61:3).

Joy means so much more than you walking around being happy. *"Therefore with joy shall ye draw water out of the wells of salvation"* (Isaiah 12:3). Joy acts as the bucket you let down into a well to draw water. The word salvation does not only mean getting saved and having eternal life as a new believer, it also means deliverance, victory, health, and divine help. When you have joy, you have a bucket to draw deliverance from different situations, that is why the scripture says, "wells of salvation," meaning there is more than one thing that you need salvation or deliverance from.

The reason many believers backslide, forsake God, and lose their salvation is because they don't have joy. Meeting God in the morning time visitation gives joy and causes you to draw salvation in the spirit. If you do not drink water for some time in the natural, you will eventually die, and it happens to your spirit man if do not have joy, your spirit man does not get waters of salvation.

"The LORD thy God in the midst of thee is mighty; he will save, ***he will rejoice over thee with joy; he will rest in his love, he will joy over thee with singing,****"* (Zephaniah 3:17).

God rejoices over you with Joy! That word rejoice means to be bright, cheerful, to exult, and display great joy. You have the potential to give great joy to the Father. Do you know how badly He wants you to get up in the morning and meet Him so you can crawl up into His womb where He can caress you with His love and show you His compassion, so you know and understand how deeply and intimately He loves you? You are the crown jewel of His creation and it gives Him great joy to see you in the fourth watch! Most of the time when you wake up early in the morning you hear a song playing in your heart because Jehovah joying and exulting over you with singing!

Joy Comes During the Morning Time Visitation

"... weeping may endure for a night, but joy cometh in the morning," (Psalm 30:5).

No matter how long you have to weep in the night, joy comes in the morning! If joy comes in the morning why then are so many Christians depressed? Joy is not just given because you are a Christian, it is given when you get up in the morning to receive your visitation. This is not the type of joy we get when we rejoice before the Lord or over some great news we receive, it is much deeper than that.

"Looking unto Jesus the author and finisher of our faith; **who for the joy that was set before him endured the cross,** *despising the shame, and is set down at the right hand of the throne of God,"* (Hebrews 12:2).

Jesus overcame the shame of the Cross because of the joy that was set before Him. The joy before Him was His future promotion to be seated at the right hand of God. The joy that Jesus had was from the anticipation and expectation of what He was going to receive when He rose from the dead, as He often spoke about to His detractors. *"... Hereafter shall ye see the Son of man sitting on the right hand of power, and coming in the clouds of heaven,"* (Matthew 26:64). The night Jesus had to pray in the garden of Gethsemane, it was a night of weeping and sorrow, but He knew joy was coming in the morning. Jesus described it to His disciples another way, when He said, *"A woman when she is in travail hath sorrow, because her hour is come: but as soon as she is delivered of the child, she remembereth no more the anguish,* **for joy that a man is born into the world,"** (John 16:21).

Jesus described the crucifixion like a woman in labor, ready to give birth. The woman is in great pain, crying out in travail as the child gets ready to come out, but when the child is born the pain is gone, and she forgets the anguish because of the joy she is holding. That is what happened to Jesus, He cried at the Cross, but He resurrected with joy in the morning.

THE WINGS OF THE MORNING

> *"**And very early in the morning** the first day of the week, they came unto the sepulchre at the rising of the sun,"* (Mark 16:2).

Jesus was not praising God because He was no longer dead, He was rejoicing because He came into His destiny and the fulfillment of everything God had for Him, all power in heaven and on earth! He had the more excellent name in God's kingdom and attained the most intimate place and position next to God the Father, the right hand of power! That was His joy, and joy belongs to your peace in the morning! He quickens you and imparts His joy to help you overcome any insurmountable and impossible situation in your life. It gives you the grace to endure whatever process God will have you go through to fulfill your destiny.

The Strength of Joy

This Joy of the Lord gives you strength! *"... **for the joy of the LORD is your strength**,"* (Nehemiah 8:10). Without the strength joy gives, you will grow weak and faint and you will not be able to deal with trials and tribulations that come in your walk with the Lord. *"**If thou faint in the day of adversity, thy strength is small**,"* (Proverbs 24:10). It is joy that gives you strength to overcome trials and tribulations and to endure hardships. Without this, you are bound to fail and fall away.

The reason why some people fall into certain temptations and weaknesses is that they lose their joy. That is why David prayed, *"**Restore unto me the joy of thy salvation...**"* (Psalm 51:12). If you feel you are losing the joy of your salvation, rise up in the morning and pray, joy will come back to you! Use the joy that comes in the morning to draw the waters of salvation that will refresh your spirit man and loose you from any kind of captivity. If you are battling demonic powers, you need the joy that comes in the morning to cripple them and cast them out of your life.

Paul and Silas used joy to get deliverance when they were arrested, beaten up, and dumped in an underground dungeon prison. *"And at midnight Paul and Silas prayed, and sang praises unto God: and the prisoners heard them,"* (Acts 16:25). Joy also comes when you begin to rejoice, praise, and sing in the midst of the trial. *"The king shall joy in thy strength, O LORD; and in thy salvation how greatly shall he rejoice!"* (Psalm 21:1). When joy comes strength comes, therefore, Paul and Silas prayed and sang praises unto God, the bucket of joy was activated, they drew fresh water out of the well of salvation, and God set them free.

"And suddenly there was a great earthquake, so that the foundations of the prison were shaken: and immediately all the doors were opened, and every one's bands were loosed," (Acts 16:26).

Joy or praise releases God to bring deliverance in your life. Paul and Silas began to rejoice in the God of their salvation and that joy brought them deliverance. An earthquake shook the foundations of that prison, opening all the doors, and breaking the chains from their hands and feet. You may be in the most dire situation you have ever encountered, but if you learn this principle and understand that when God comes with joy in the morning, you will draw out of the wells of salvation and get your deliverance.

Plants Grow in the Morning
God's Breath Causes All Vegetation to Grow

When God visits the earth, He breathes on all vegetation causing it to sprout, flourish, and blossom during the fourth watch, and that includes you. You are a type of a plant too, so when God visits the earth, things in your life flourish and blossom if you rise up to meet Him in the morning visitation!

"... in the morning they are like grass which groweth up. In the morning it flourisheth, and groweth up," (Psalm 90:5-6).

The word "morning" is *boqer* meaning "dawn as the break of day," at dawn, early in the morning plants grow, spring up, or sprout, and they flourish or flower. Seeds are also sown in the morning. *"In the morning sow thy seed..."* (Ecclesiastes 11:6). Why does this happen when God visits the earth? Because He releases His breath and the plants spring up and flower!

THE WINGS OF THE MORNING

> *"Thou sendest forth thy spirit, they are created: and thou renewest the face of the earth,"* (Psalm 104:30).

The easy-to-read version of the Bible translates this same verse as follows **"But when you send out your life-giving breath, things come alive, and the world is like new again!"** (Psalm 104:30). When God comes from heaven He breathes or blows on the earth and creatively renews the *"face of the earth,"* It is the breath of God that gives life to the whole earth. *"The Spirit of God hath made me,* **and the breath of the Almighty hath given me life,"** (Job 33:4). Every morning God comes on earth, bends over, and blows with His mouth releasing His breath across the face of the earth. Everything growing on the earth grows supernaturally, it's not natural for plants to grow and spring forth, it is supernatural because God does it!

When I was a child in Memphis, Tennessee I had a garden. I was extremely curious as a child and I was always fascinated with how cucumbers and watermelons grew. I would wake up early in the morning and run outside to see how much they grew overnight. I was amazed at how the little yellow flowers on them would blossom and then close up later in the day. I sat gazing intently at a plant, trying to capture the moment when the buds would blossom and the plants would grow, but I never saw anything happen. Nevertheless, the next day when I rushed out to see the plants, some type of change or transformation always took place. All those memories flooded my mind when I started studying and searching the scriptures for all the things that happen during the morning time visitation, and the Lord said, *"David, do you know that when you put a watermelon seed in the ground, I am the one who makes it grow? One day it is in the ground and another day shoots appear above the ground. You don't see the plants growing, but I am the one blowing and causing them to grow and spring forth in the morning when I visit the earth."*

God comes down every morning and breathes life into creation every day, if He doesn't, nothing would exist. *"Thou hidest thy face, they are troubled: thou takest away their breath, they die, and return to their dust,"* (Psalm 104:29). If God stops giving us life we will die. Contrary to what people think, creation cannot exist on its own. *"For in him we live, and move, and have our being ..."* (Acts 17:28). Everything lives, moves, and exists because of Him! *"He watereth the hills from his chambers: the earth is satisfied with the fruit of thy works,"* (Psalm 104:13). The earth depends on God to water and sustain it every day with the dew of Heaven.

Scientists are still wondering how and why plants grow in the night and in the hours before dawn. According to sciencedaily.com, scientists realize that plants "...actually grow in spurts late at night, with plant stems elongating fastest in the hours just before dawn." While scientists are wondering, we already know. Every morning God visits the earth, He breathes on creation making it come to life and grow. If you put a camera on a plant throughout the night you will see them growing between 3 a.m. until the sun rises. It is miraculous! Only God makes seeds grow and plants blossom.

"And he said, So is the kingdom of God, as if a man should cast seed into the ground; And should sleep, and rise night and day, ***and the seed should spring and grow up, he knoweth not how,****"* (Mark 4:26-27).

God Uses a Plant to Rebuke Jonah

Jonah was disobedient to God, and instead of going to Nineveh to give a word to that city as God instructed, he went on a ship to Tarshish. During that voyage, God sent a storm that almost destroyed the ship. The mariners solved the problem by throwing the disobedient prophet overboard and the sea calmed down. *"Now the LORD had prepared a great fish to swallow up Jonah. And Jonah was in the belly of the fish three days and three nights"* (Jonah 1:17). This verse confirms that God deals with animals to do His will when He visits the earth. Animals know and understand God, they did in the beginning before Adam fell, and they still do.

After three days, Jonah repented and the great fish vomited him on the shores of Nineveh and he prophesied to Nineveh that God was going to destroy the city in 40 days. The people of Nineveh repented and humbled themselves with fasting when they heard the prophecy, and their repentance caused God to change His mind, which embarrassed Jonah and he took offense. God came up with a plan to teach Jonah a lesson.

> *"And the LORD **God prepared a gourd,** and made it to come up over Jonah, that it might be a shadow over his head, to deliver him from his grief. So Jonah was exceeding glad of the gourd. But **God prepared a worm when the morning rose the next day,** and it smote the gourd that it withered,"* (Jonah 4:6-7).

A gourd is a palmcrist plant that produces castor oil. The Treasury of Scriptural Knowledge defines a gourd as follows, "It is as large as the olive tree, has leaves like those of a vine, sometimes as broad as the brim of a hat, and is of very quick growth." According to Psalm 90:5-6, plants grow up and flourish in the morning, therefore, God must have prepared the gourd early in the morning to be a shade over Jonah and he was very happy to be shielded. After the rapid growth and shade, God prepared a worm to destroy the plant, to deal with the religious and judgmental attitude of Jonah.

The worm ate the plant and Jonah's shade was gone. When the sun came up it was beating on Jonah's exposed head, to complicate things more, a strong, dry, east wind blew on him, causing him to faint. Jonah was distressed by the situation and wanted to die, at which point God rebuked Jonah because he had more compassion for a plant than for the people and livestock of Nineveh!

All plants and herbs grow supernaturally and increase without us noticing, because we are often asleep when it happens, which is a manifestation of God's meekness. Peter describes a meek heart as the *"hidden man of the heart."* God does His work in secret and in the hidden invisible realm

We think it is sunlight that makes plants grow, but it is really God. Sunlight has a role in the continual growth and development of the plant, but it is in the morning when God visits the earth that causes the plants to spring forth and blossom! Only God has the power to make anything grow. *"Which of you by taking thought can add one cubit unto his stature?"* (Matthew 6:27). God can take a hard seed that is planted in dirt and turn it into a flower that bears fruit. That is what I call a miracle of creation!

You Are a Tree and a Planting of the Lord

The revelation of this mystery is that God is not simply interested in plants and animals, He comes down here for you, His prized possession. You are the apple of His eye! Because His heart is set on you, when He comes on earth, He commands the morning, creation, and everything else to serve you. Just as vegetation grows, flourishes, and flowers in the morning, you do too! The Bible says, **"...ye are God's husbandry, ye are God's building,"** (1 Corinthians 3:9). Husbandry in this context means a planting or a garden. God sees you as a garden and a plant that has to be watered and cultivated.

> *"... and in his law doth he meditate day and night.* ***And he shall be like a tree planted by the rivers of water, that bringeth forth his fruit in his season; his leaf also shall not wither;*** *and whatsoever he doeth shall prosper,"* (Psalm 1:2-3).

> *"To appoint unto them that mourn in Zion ...* ***that they might be called trees of righteousness, the planting of the LORD,*** *that he might be glorified,"* (Isaiah 61:3).

> *"Blessed is the man that trusteth in the LORD, and whose hope the LORD is.* ***For he shall be as a tree planted by the waters, and that spreadeth out her roots by the river,*** *and shall not see when heat cometh,* ***but her leaf shall be green;*** *and shall not be careful in the year of drought,* ***neither shall cease from yielding fruit,"*** *(Jeremiah 17:7-8).*

You are a tree planted by rivers of water with roots, leaves, and fruit! You are a tree of righteousness! You are a planting of the Lord! Jesus also speaks of men as being either good or bad trees. **"A good tree cannot bring forth evil fruit, neither can a corrupt tree bring forth good fruit.**

Every tree that bringeth not forth good fruit is hewn down, and cast into the fire. Wherefore by their fruits ye shall know them," (Matthew 7:18-20).

"The righteous shall flourish like the palm tree: he shall grow like a cedar in Lebanon," (Psalm 92:12).

Many saints are dried up, worn out, and withered in their body because they do not know what belongs to their peace in the morning time visitation. When you rise up to meet God in the fourth watch you spring up, you flourish, you blossom, you flower in life, becoming fruitful and productive!

The Lord once said to me, *"David tell my people, if I visit creation every morning and cause seeds to grow and flourish, when they get up to meet me at that time, I will do the same in their life."* The Lord wants you to know that when you enter the womb of the morning, He will cause you to grow and flourish in life. He will breathe on whatever seed He has planted in you to cause it to start growing and creative abilities will begin to blossom. Things you wanted God to do and have cried out and prayed for to happen, but have not, will miraculously take place when you rise in the morning to meet God.

God will breathe on you and things that are dead or dying in your life, will be renewed and resurrected, and you will spring forth! You will experience healing and rejuvenation in your spirit, soul, and body every time you meet God in the morning.

God Manifests His Lovingkindness in the Morning
God Commands His Loving Kindness in the Daytime, but it Manifests at Dawn

"To shew forth thy lovingkindness in the morning, and thy faithfulness every night," (Psalm 92:2).

God's lovingkindness manifests early in the morning, and it's one of the first things you hear when God awakens your ear. *"Cause me to hear thy lovingkindness in the morning; for in thee do I trust ..."* (Psalm 143:8). Before every day is over, God already commands which loving kindness He wants to give you when you wake up to meet Him in the morning.

"Yet the LORD will command his lovingkindness in the daytime..."
(Psalm 42:8).

One thing you must understand is that God does specific things at different times of the day and night. God commands His lovingkindness in the daytime or during the day, but He manifests what He commands at dawn, early in the morning when He visits the earth. Commanding something and manifesting it are two different things. God commands His loving kindness then He shows it.

Understanding Lovingkindness

Lovingkindness is a manifestation of God's mercy toward you. Lovingkindness means kindness, favor, good deeds, and mercy. The root word for "lovingkindness" is *chasad* which means to bow the neck only, not the knee, to be kind, to reprove, mercy. Every time God visits you in the morning, He bows His neck to you. For the King of the whole world to do that to you is major because usually, you are the one who has to kneel to the king. When you rise up in the morning to meet Him, you get His attention and He displays His kindness to you in a loving way. He bows His neck to you saying, *"I am pleased with you, I am showing you My lovingkindness."*

The lovingkindness of God is not only a matter of obligation but also of generosity, and not only of loyalty, but mercy. The weaker party in any relationship seeks protection and blessings from the stronger, who is God. The stronger party remains committed to His promises but retains the freedom to determine the manner in which He implements His promises. Lovingkindness implies the personal involvement of God in your life, and His commitment to a relationship, beyond the rule of law.

God's lovingkindness means that even if you mess up, He is still obligated to show you His kindness beyond the rule of law. The law is cut and dry, and when you break it, you have to be punished. *"For whosoever shall keep the whole law, and yet offend in one point, he is guilty of all,"* (James 2:10). However, God's lovingkindness flows from the relationship, not the law. When you mess up, God's lovingkindness reproves and rebukes you for what you did, but then passes you on. If God did not do that, you would never receive any of the promises He has for you, because the law kills you. For that reason, lovingkindness is not just by obligation, rules, or the law, but also by mercy.

This is very good to know because all of us are fallen at our best as Romans 3:10 says, *"As it is written, There is none righteous, no, not one."* If we did not have God's lovingkindness we would be lost forever. But when you get up in the morning you receive the nod from God, you receive His lovingkindness. And this love goes beyond how much right or wrong you have done because He is not committed to doing this for you out of obligation. He is committed to do this for you based on loyalty and love. His personal involvement and commitment to you flow out a relationship beyond the rule or the law. Do not let anyone make you think that because you did something wrong God is no longer with you. That's a lie. Jesus said, *"... I will never leave thee, nor forsake thee."* (Heb 13:5) Jesus keeps His personal involvement in your life not because you have obeyed every rule but because He's loving and He's kind. That is His lovingkindness and goodness to you.

The Reproof of Lovingkindness

Part of God's lovingkindness to you in the morning is Him rebuking and correcting you. **"Let the righteous smite me; it shall be a kindness:** *and let him reprove me; it shall be an excellent oil, which shall not break my head..."* (Psalm 141:5) God's correction will not destroy you, because He remains loving and kind, even when He corrects harshly. David calls the reproof of God *"an excellent oil,"* an anointing, an enduement of power, that will not break his head!

We think correction is a bad thing, but every time God brings a reproof, correction, or an adjustment in your life, He is nodding at you, He is pleased with you and showing you His lovingkindness by pouring oil on your head! When God rebukes you, He is exercising His loving kindness to you. God is so kind that even if you do not rise up to meet Him in the fourth watch, He goes the extra mile and gives you a dream of warning and chastens you in your sleep, to keep you from making a wrong move!

> *"For God speaketh once, yea twice, yet man perceiveth it not.* ***In a dream, in a vision of the night, when deep sleep falleth upon men,*** *in slumberings upon the bed; Then he openeth the ears of men, and sealeth their instruction, That he may withdraw man from his purpose, and hide pride from man.* ***He keepeth back his soul from the pit, and his life from perishing by the sword. He is chastened also with pain upon his bed,*** *and the multitude of his bones with strong pain,"* (Job 33:14-19).

In God's lovingkindness, He reproofs and chastens to keep you from dying and going to the pit of hell! For that reason, you must love His chastening and correction, and always remember it is His lovingkindness. When the Lord does this, He is saying, *"I am still personally involved and committed to you beyond the rule of law."* We need to really understand this, because God is not like people who breach contracts and relationships are broken. His love goes beyond what He knows about us, His love and kindness remain.

God Brings Justice to Light Every Morning
He Hears Your Case in the Morning

> *"The just LORD is in the midst thereof; he will not do iniquity:* ***every morning doth he bring his judgment to light,*** *he faileth not; but the unjust knoweth no shame,"* (Zephaniah 3:5).

Without fail, God's justice is another thing that belongs to your peace morning by morning. When you wake up to meet Him early in the morning, you can expect Him to faithfully bring judgment in your life. He is an acting potentate or a judge upon a seat, to hear your case, and bring a verdict. He will sit in judgment over your situation and maintain your cause. One of the blessings of the morning is that God will hear your case. If you want your case to be heard, get up in the morning, and He will bring your justice to light every morning!

"O house of David, thus saith the LORD; **Execute judgment in the morning,** *and deliver him that is spoiled out of the hand of the oppressor, lest my fury go out like fire, and burn that none can quench it, because of the evil of your doings,"* (Jeremiah 21:12).

If God expects you to execute judgment in the morning, you can be sure that He does the same. Every morning He executes judgment for you. If you are being treated unjustly, God will bring a verdict for you (Psalm 35:7). When you get up in the morning, He will awaken for you and hear your case. Right where you are, say, *"Father, thank you for being just! Thank you for bringing justice to light in my life every morning when I rise up to meet you!"*

Overcoming the Accuser of the Brethren

"... for the accuser of our brethren is cast down, which accused them before our God day and night," (Revelation 12:10).

The question we must ask ourselves is, why does God do this every morning? It is because Satan, the accuser of the brethren, diligently goes to the courts of heaven with accusations, slander, and judgments against you, every day. If you do not realize that God brings your judgment to light, His verdict, and His lovingkindness in the morning, to overrule every accusation Satan brings, you will suffer loss.

If you are not diligent in meeting God in the morning to deal with these accusations, you can suffer indictments and warrants in the spirit that can greatly hinder your life. Be diligent to clear yourself when a judgment is brought against you.

"*Agree with thine adversary quickly, whiles thou art in the way with him;* *lest at any time the* ***adversary deliver thee to the judge, and the judge deliver thee to the officer, and thou be cast into prison.*** *Verily I say unto*

> *thee, Thou shalt by no means come out thence, till thou hast paid the uttermost farthing,"* (Matthew 5:25-26).

To agree with the adversary means to make every effort to resolve any judgment or charge made against you, otherwise you will be brought before the judge, and imprisoned. When you are imprisoned in the spirit, you remain incarcerated until every issue about the case is thoroughly resolved, which can result in years of stagnation and delay. For these reasons, you must discern the timing of God's visitation in the morning or you will suffer loss, warfare, and desolation, like Israel did when they missed the Messianic Visitation.

God visits you every morning with justice, loving kindness, new mercies, and His compassions are faithfully released in your life so that you are not consumed. His justice preserves your life and destiny. If you miss His morning visitation, you miss the things He brings to give to you. Every time you rise to meet the Lord, even if you are wrong and fully deserving of judgment, He rebukes the accuser and drives Him from your life. God gives you a nod and renders judgment in your favor as He did for Joshua.

> *"And he shewed me Joshua the high priest standing before the angel of the LORD,* **and Satan standing at his right hand to resist him. And the LORD said unto Satan, The LORD rebuke thee,** *O Satan; even the LORD that hath chosen Jerusalem rebuke thee: is not this a brand plucked out of the fire?"* (Zechariah 3:1-2).

The Lord does not apply this to the spiritual realm only, when Satan brings charges against you in natural courts, God will hear your case and bring justice to light. Too many believers depend on good lawyers to get their cases resolved in the courts of men, but God can overrule earthly judges because He is the judge of the whole earth. Getting a good lawyer is great, but you can do better as a believer, if you meet God in the morning, He will turn things around for you.

"Who shall lay any thing to the charge of God's elect? It is God that justifieth," (Romans 8:33).

Personal Testimonies of God Bringing Justice to Light
A Young Man Dies After Suing Me in Court

If you yield to the mercy of an earthly judge, you can lose because they can be wrong and unjust. However, when you get up early and go before the God of justice and let Him hear your case, even if you are wrong, He will have mercy and justify you. This is how God brings your justice to light and maintains your cause.

In my early days, when I started meeting God in morning time visitation prayer, I didn't know He was sitting as a judge over every case people brought against me. Early in my ministry, I had a big crusade in St. Louis. God moved marvelously and many people received healing and other amazing miracles. A young man was healed of sickle cell disease without me laying hands on him. He and his wife were brought on stage to share the healing testimony. While they were on stage with me, the Lord revealed something very serious that was going on in their marriage and told me to reveal it openly. The whole family was blessed and set free.

The service was live-streamed and his pastor was watching. He had a problem with the way I ministered to the young man and his family and said, *"Why did he air you live like that? You need to sue him and his ministry."* The next thing we knew, we were being sued by the man who received supernatural healing and deliverance in my crusade. I sent this message to him. *"You don't need to do this it is very bad and dangerous. You must understand I don't have a ministry like a normal prophet or apostle where God can judge you for touching the anointing, that is a lower realm than what I am operating in. In my ministry Jesus Himself personally works with me one on one. My ministry is not based on an anointing, it is from a face to face relationship with Jesus."* I explained to him how the Lord works with me personally and why that makes what he was doing very dangerous. I strongly encouraged him to reconsider what he was doing. I repeated, *"It is very dangerous for you to do this."*

What Happens in the Morning

I was not trying to frighten him, and I was not afraid of going to court. I do not like courts because they are not the place for preachers to be. Paul exhorted the churches under him not to take their cases to secular courts but to have the elders in the church resolve them. For that reason, I believe we should avoid courts as much as possible. At the time I was being sued, I was getting up in the morning and presenting my case before the Lord, telling Him about the court date coming up, what the young man was doing, and how it could hinder my ministry. As I continued meeting God in morning prayer, I was becoming very concerned for the young man's life. I kept feeling a danger in my spirit and I didn't want anything evil to happen to him.

I sent another message to him, *"Please don't do this."* A pastor on my staff knew him and went to talk to him, but because of what his pastor said, he wouldn't listen and pursued with the case. It is amazing how demonic some pastors are. I stopped reaching out to him and left everything in God's hands, because He is in control and works all things out for good. Even in times when I made mistakes and was wrong, God protected the face to face movement because it is not my ministry, it is His! Jesus is personally over my ministry, and if you notice, I don't call it "David E. Taylor Ministries." God said to me, *"You are part of my destiny now. I want you to lead the face to face movement and tell the elders of the church what is going on. Tell them to come out of their camps to meet with me."* This move is bigger than a man's ministry. It is God's move on the earth.

A week and a half later the young man had an accident and was decapitated and died instantly, the case was thrown out of court. The Lord maintained my case and brought justice to light in my life. This man was too young to die, but God does not care about that. He will kill you if He has to. I know that sounds harsh but it is the truth. The church is sadly ignorant about the ways of the Lord.

> *"See now that I, even I, am he, and there is no god with me: **I kill, and I make alive; I wound, and I heal: neither is there any that can deliver out of my hand,**"* (Deuteronomy 32:39).

God is good and full of mercy and compassion, but as a just judge, He will kill people, young or old. Indeed, *"It is a fearful thing to fall into the hands of the living God"* (Hebrews 10:31). It is bad enough to come against an anointed man of God because the Bible says, *"touch not my anointed and do my prophets no harm."* However, it is much worse to come against a ministry that is working with the Lord face to face. The consequences of coming against a face to face ministry are dreadful. Jesus warned the Jews about fearing God the Father.

"And fear not them which kill the body, but are not able to kill the soul: ***but rather fear him which is able to destroy both soul and body in hell,"***
(Matthew 10:28).

This is the kind of glory that God is birthing in the earth today, it will set order and even make politicians and government officials, tremble. **"Behold therefore the goodness and severity of God:** *on them which fell, severity; but toward thee, goodness..."* (Romans 11:22). God is good but He is also severe, and you must get understanding of both sides. In America, there is no fear of God, people walk into His house and mistreat His leaders irreverently. However, that is changing because the Father is spearheading the glory move Himself!

There are also religious leaders and modern-day Pharisees who think they can treat other officers and men of God badly and without consequence, but they are deceived. You cannot disrespect and dishonor another officer, especially if they are of greater rank than you, because it is equalizing. God hates a religious and equalizing spirit and it will not go unpunished.

God Judges Leaders for Trying to Destroy My Ministry

No matter who you are or what kind of relationship you think you have with God, you must understand rank and the mystery of authority. There were at least eight national leaders who conspired to hurt my ministry and were on their way to the news media. These are church leaders you would know if I mentioned their names. This is the kind of persecution I face continually with leaders. They have tried to use other people to destroy the ministry God gave me, and failed, and this time they were going to stir up a major accusation against me. I had no idea what was going on until one of them, who was totally against me, called weeping.

I was extremely surprised, because I knew of his intense opposition to the face to face call on my life. I gingerly picked up the phone and he was sobbing and crying, and said, *"David, I'm sorry – I'm not going to do this."* I said, *"What are you talking about?"* Then he told me how he and some major leaders were planning to go to the media to do a hit job on me. He said, *"David, last night Jesus came to me in a dream and sternly rebuked me and told me to leave you alone. He was in a beautiful white robe and He told me that He loves you very much and if I didn't stop coming after you, I would be judged and killed."* Needless to say, Jesus appearing to one of the ring leaders stopped the whole attack and caused justice to come to light for me in the morning!

You must understand that to attack an officer of a higher rank can be disastrous to your life and destiny. By the Spirit, Paul encouraged believers to be subject to higher powers. *"Whosoever therefore resisteth the power, resisteth the ordinance of God: and they that resist shall receive to themselves damnation,"* (Romans 13:2). God is on the earth working with me in the Face to Face Movement, this is not an ordinary ministry, therefore to resist it is very dangerous, because it is resisting God Himself. I have seen judges, police chiefs, and mayors of cities judged for coming against me, because I know what belongs to my peace in the morning.

The Judgments of God Set Order

It is not my heart to share these testimonies to scare anyone, but to remind the Church and America that we need the fear of God to be restored in our hearts and lives. People do not reverence the Lord as in days past and He is coming on earth to set order. They may not respect and honor the church, but they will fear God. He will make sure of that in the latter rain glory move. He will do things to create fear, not fleshly fear or the wrong kind of fear that has torment, the clean pure fear of God.

"The fear of the LORD is clean, enduring for ever: the judgments of the LORD are true and righteous altogether," (Psalm 19:9).

The God kind of fear is produced by His judgments, sets boundaries, and establishes order. *"... yea, with my spirit within me will I seek thee early: for when thy judgments are in the earth, the inhabitants of the world will learn righteousness,"* (Isaiah 26:9). God's judgments will cause the world to learn righteousness. Isaiah sought God early in the morning when His judgments hit the earth. In the Acts of the Apostles, the fear of God hit Jerusalem when people started dying. Ananias and Sapphira died, and Herod was even struck by an angel, and died a horrible death, for attacking the lives of the apostles.

God is setting order by bringing judgment and government to the whole world. God told Moses to rise early and go to Pharaoh to pronounce His judgments, because when you rise early in the morning, God is your justice. When you get into this kind of relationship with the Lord you are protected. I am not saying I have been right about everything, but that is what His lovingkindness and justice is for!

God Fights for You in the Morning
He Fought for Israel in the Morning

*"And it came to pass, **that in the morning watch the LORD looked unto the host of the Egyptians through the pillar of fire and of the cloud, and troubled the host of the Egyptians,** And took off their chariot wheels, that they drave them heavily: so that the Egyptians said, Let us flee from the face of Israel; **for the LORD fighteth for them against the Egyptians.** And the LORD said unto Moses, Stretch out thine hand over the sea, that the waters may come again upon the Egyptians, upon their chariots, and upon their horsemen,"* (Exodus 14:24-26).

When God visits the earth, He fights for those who rise up to meet with Him. God had to make a way for the Israelites to flee Egypt.

What Happens in the Morning

Therefore, with the rod of God in his hand, Moses divided the sea and they crossed. The Egyptian army was hot on their heels, and when they followed after the Israelites, Jehovah peeked through the pillar of fire and of the cloud and confused the Egyptian army and took the wheels off of their chariots!

The Egyptians saw the face of God when He looked through the pillar of the cloud and they said, *"... Let us flee from the face of Israel; for the LORD fighteth for them against the Egyptians,"* (Exodus 14:25). The people in Moses' day saw God's face in the clouds, just as people are seeing Him today, as He works with me.

God was not done with the Egyptians. *"And Moses stretched forth his hand over the sea,* **and the sea returned to his strength when the morning appeared;** *and the Egyptians fled against it; and the LORD overthrew the Egyptians in the midst of the sea,"* (Exodus 14:27).

God drowned the Egyptians "when the morning (dawn) appeared," because there is a divine spiritual law that gives the upright dominion over the wicked in the morning (Psalm 49:14)! When you rise up to meet God in the fourth watch, people that are fighting against you, attacking your reputation and integrity, and making false accusations and charges against you, will experience God fighting against them!

This is also part of the covenant of the sure mercies of David. *"The enemy shall not exact upon him; nor the son of wickedness afflict him.* **And I will beat down his foes before his face,** *and plague them that hate him,"* (Psalm 89:22-23). God defended David at dawn, and He will do the same for you. God confronts your enemies early in the morning.

CHAPTER 10
The Womb of the Morning

CHAPTER 10
The Womb of the Morning

Cherished in the Womb of the Morning

Morning time prayer also gives you access to God's womb. It is the place where He cherishes, nurtures, and faithfully takes care of you. David understood the fourth watch mystery and the womb of the morning because he mastered the morning time visitation.

*"Thy people shall be willing in the day of thy power, in the beauties of **holiness from the womb of the morning:** thou hast the dew of thy youth,"*
(Psalm 110:3).

When we talk about God's womb of the morning, I want you to imagine a pregnant woman rubbing her hands on her belly, lovingly caressing the unborn child inside her. When you really access God's womb, you experience His overwhelming love and compassion for you. The morning time is when God just wants to rub your head and tell you how much He loves you, just like natural fathers do to their little babies (1 John 4:16).

Every time I enter this realm and get deep in prayer, tears start flowing from my eyes as the Father's love pours over me. It is so overwhelmingly powerful and awesome. If you rise early and pray at 3 a.m. until daybreak you will experience God's deep love for you and receive the capacity to love. *"We love him, because he first loved us,"* (1 John 4:19). Without God loving you first you cannot love right. Your love walk depends on the great mercies you receive when God visits you in the morning.

Experiencing God's Compassions in the Morning

> *"... in the beauties of holiness from the womb of the morning: thou hast the dew of thy youth,"* (Psalm 110:3).

To understand the revelation of the womb of the morning, we need to define it in Hebrew, which is *rechem* with the root *racham*, which according to the Strong's Concordance means "to love, to fondle, to compassionate, to have compassion on or upon, to have mercy, to pity." The womb means "to love deeply with great compassion." The Hebrew word *racham* also means "compassion, the womb as cherishing the fetus, bowels."

When you say the womb of the morning you are basically saying that the morning time is the place God cherishes us and His compassion moves on our behalf. The womb also carries the meaning of how the bowels of a woman are stirred up when her baby cries. That is what happens when one is filled with compassion, like Jesus was when He saw the sick coming to Him. *"And Jesus went forth, and saw a great multitude, **and was moved with compassion toward them,** and he healed their sick,"* (Matthew 14:14). Out of His compassion, power flowed to heal and deliver the sick and oppressed.

God loves everybody but He does not move for everybody. If you get up in the morning, He will give you unfailing compassions, not just love. You can love people and do nothing for them. His compassions are new every morning which means they are available to you when you get up for fourth watch prayer. There are saints who have lost their children in car accidents or experienced other disasters, and they ask God, *"Why did you allow this to happen? I'm saved, I am a Christian. How could this happen to me?"* The real question is, *"Were you getting up in the morning to meet God when He visits man? Were you receiving the new mercies He has for you every morning and the blessings of the morning time visitation prayer that He wanted to give for your peace?"* When you miss your time of visitation, you lose your peace.

I want you to gain a deep appreciation for what happens when Jesus visits you in the morning. The womb of the morning is the place of the Lord's compassions and when He cherishes and comforts us with His love like a mother does to the fetus in her womb or her newborn.

> *"It is of the LORD'S mercies that we are not consumed, **because his compassions fail not.** They are new every morning: great is thy faithfulnesss,"* (Lamentations 3:22-23).

Have you ever felt what I am describing to you when you pray early in the morning? I have met many who have. When I teach about the mystery of the morning time visitation prayer, many come and confirm what I am sharing with you now. They say, *"I spent time with God this morning and He told me how precious and special I was to Him."* When I ask them when they prayed, they say, *"In the morning between 3 and 6 a.m.,"* and I tell them they were in God's womb and receiving His love!

Why Your Love Gets Cold

Everyone needs the divine prenatal care from God in the womb of the morning because a fresh fervent dose of His love will keep your love from getting cold. ***"... the love of many shall wax cold,"*** (Matthew 24:12). Your heart grows cold when you miss the morning time visitation where His "compassions," deep love, and affections are available for you to receive.

I know preachers who have been in ministry for years who stopped spending time with God especially in the mornings, become cold and hard, and they run their ministry like a business because they lack the love they once had for God. *"Nevertheless I have somewhat against thee, because thou hast left thy first love,"* (Revelation 2:4). Many ministers have lost their first love, not that they don't love Him, but their love is covered up with so much hardness because they do not make time to meet God in the morning, so He can cherish and love on them. In this time, God comforts and cherishes you, and He removes the callousness, so you develop a tender heart.

You can only love right when God first loves you. *"We love him, because he first loved us,"* (1 John 4:19). If you don't get inside the womb of the morning, where God can love you first, you will not have the softness and tenderness of heart to give love back to Him or others. Ministry will become like a war zone for you and it will make you bitter and hard-hearted. It is vital that you focus more on your relationship with God than on ministry. Ministry should flow from the relationship you have with Him.

With great sorrow, I have watched many leaders become hardened and calloused because no one can love God on his own. God sheds His love into your heart before you can walk in love. I must emphasize that you cannot love God until He has loved you, therefore, you must stay in the womb of the morning.

The Church must stay in the womb of the morning otherwise she will become religious and lapse into tradition like the Pharisees and Sadducees of Jesus' day. Church services will just become a social and religious activity. I am not saying this from a point of perfection, I have experienced seasons when I didn't feel the love of God and my heart grew cold and hard. I could not feel any tenderness in my heart, and it was harder to weep in worship.

When you have been cherished and nourished in the womb of God's love, you become so tenderhearted. In the evening, the moment you enter the courts of God and you feel His touch on your heart, you begin to weep. It is not hard for Him to get through to you, because the womb softens your heart. *"And the LORD thy God will circumcise thine heart, and the heart of thy seed, to love the LORD thy God with all thine heart, and with all thy soul, that thou mayest live,"* (Deuteronomy 30:6). The womb of the morning is where God circumcises your heart so you can love right.

Why Preachers Grow Cold

Part of my global mandate as an emperor is to counsel leaders all over the world. They keep saying, *"David, I don't understand my relationship with God. I don't feel the love I once had for Him."* One of them said, *"Ministry has become so difficult. I have been betrayed so many times in my church."* They confess and share a litany of issues with me, because I cover a lot of bishops, fivefold ministers, and churches.

Another leader came to me very broken and honest, and said, *"I've been in ministry 30 years and I have lost my fire for God. I've lost my first love. What am I to do? I don't want to feel like this. I know I love God, but through the years this ministry has hardened me."* This is what happens to many minsters, they get so busy working for God, that they forget to spend time with Him. Ministry without intimacy with God makes you hard, cold, and religious, and your love and compassion toward people is not the way it should be.

"And be ye kind one to another, tenderhearted, forgiving one another, *even as God for Christ's sake hath forgiven you,"* (Ephesians 4:32).

How can you be kind and tenderhearted when you do not frequent the womb of God? How can you love when you have not first experienced love? Many believers cannot love each other in the church because they are not getting cherished by God in the morning. You must have that love flowing over your life and heart so it can become tender to love others. Without this, you become calloused and ministry becomes an activity, a job, and it becomes boring.

Many ministers are leaving ministry, and some are even committing suicide. They say, *"This is not what I signed up for, I didn't know it would be like this."* What is really happening is that the tender and loving heart they had at the beginning has become cold because they were not being cherished in the womb of the morning. When you are loved on every morning by God, you feel valued and special and are strengthened to get up and do it again. If you go for days, weeks, and months without visiting God's womb to get this special love and compassion, you grow cold, but you can reverse it by entering the womb of the morning and receive the depths of God's love.

The Womb of the Morning: A Birthing Place

When you spend time with God in the morning it is like you are crawling into His womb, letting Him love you. David said, *"Cause me to hear thy lovingkindness in the morning ..."* (Psalm 143:8). Every time you pray in the morning you are in the place were God grooms you, grows you, covers you, and protects you in a special way because He is birthing you for destiny!

I believe if you rise early in the morning and pray until daybreak for nine months, something new will be birthed in your life. God's bosom is another place in Him where a child or newborn is cherished and comforted, but the womb is where a fetus is cherished. These are two different places and realms in God correspond to different phases of your spiritual growth and development. When you get up in the morning and spend time with God, you are not going under the shadow of the Almighty or the bosom of the Almighty, you are going into His belly. You can only enter the womb of God in the morning.

The womb of the morning is a place where we need to get in and stay until we are totally renewed, rebuilt, restored, made whole, and are ready to be birthed! It is the place where you grow and mature like an embryo in a mother's womb. The morning time visitation prayer is not just a wing that transports you spiritually to your destiny, it is also a womb that births you into your destiny.

"Thy people shall be willing in the day of thy power, in the beauties of holiness from the womb of the morning: thou hast the dew of thy youth,"
(Psalm 110:3).

The beauties of holiness are birthed in your lifestyle and character through the womb of the morning! If you want to bear fruit in your character enter God's womb in the morning and you will see changes. Jacob's devious and deceptive character was changed when an angel wrestled with him all night, and he received a name change and transformed character at the breaking of day!

Psalm 110:3 also talks about the day of your power being birthed out of the womb of the morning. I found when you get up in the morning time there is supernatural enablement birthed in your life that causes you to flourish. You do not even need to pray for it, you just have to be up in the morning is when the Heavens are open for God to do things He normally would not do unless you get up in the morning.

Some ministries have not gotten off the ground because they have not been incubated in the womb of the morning, where God births prophetic ministries through morning prayer. A lot of people want to be apostles, prophets, and prophetesses, but they do not want to pay the price to get up early in the morning. If you have a prophetic call on your life, then you must understand the morning time is the key to you being sent by God. If you don't get up in the morning, God has not sent you. *"I have not sent these prophets, yet they ran: I have not spoken to them, yet they prophesied,"* (Jeremiah 23:21). God births prophets and their ministries from the womb of the morning.

There are many nights that I get up and go to the sanctuary to pray at 3 a.m., and Jesus openly appears to me because He meets with men on earth at the time. When you miss the morning time, you are in danger of walking under a closed heaven, and certain things you desire, and need cannot manifest unless they are birthed during fourth watch prayer. Morning time prayer opens the heavens and things you desire begin to manifest in your life.

CHAPTER 11
Royal Power of a Prince

CHAPTER 11
Royal Power of a Prince

Morning Prayer Makes You a Prince with God
You Come into Royal Power in the Fourth Watch

Like it was with Jacob, when he was made a prince, God will give you royal power in the morning. Most believers do not know how important and significant it is for God to do this. Satan has demonic princes that rule in every city, therefore, in the fourth watch prayer, God raising up princes from His house to rule cities as well! He is raising Pastors up that will come into this royal power and do greater than what the demonic forces are doing in theirs!

The Holy Spirit releases royal anointings and priestly anointings. The anointing of the apostle, prophet, evangelist, pastor, and teacher all operate in the priestly realm, and pertain to the house of God. *"And God hath set some in the church, first apostles, secondarily prophets, thirdly teachers ..."* (1 Corinthians 12:28). The offices God has set in the church are priestly anointings and powers. However, the royal anointings go beyond the House of God, they are anointings and powers of princes, kings, and emperors. These officers know how to rule outside the house of God, they take over cities and bring regional transformation!

Until you know your identity in the Kingdom, your powers against certain demonic powers are primitive, and explains why the church has not dealt with demons who rule certain regions because they have tried facing a demonic kingdom with a church anointing, and that does not work. It takes a kingdom to fight a kingdom. You cannot fight a prince demon with a priestly anointing. The Bible calls certain demons princes, such as the prince of the power of the air, who works through children of disobedience, and princes of the world that rule entire regions (1 Corinthians 2:8; Ephesians 2:2). Jesus referred to demon princes as strongmen and they rule strongholds known as principalities or palaces. You cannot fight these evil spirits with a priestly or preacher's anointing. You need to walk in the royal anointing of a king to break these spirits.

You are a King and a Priest

"And hath made us kings and priests unto God ..." (Revelation 1:6).

I need you to understand that when God created you, He made you a king and a priest. To help you understand what I am sharing, imagine two charts: an identity chart of who you are in the church realm and an identity chart of who you are in the kingdom. The identity chart in the church covers the fivefold ministry offices and ranks, which are the priestly realm and they include: apostles, prophets, evangelists, pastors, and teachers. There are also bishops.

The identity chart in the kingdom is not quite like that. God did not create a chart for the Kingdom as clearly as He did for the church. He hid the Kingdom chart in the Bible because it is hidden and shrouded in both revelation and mystery. Revelations are high truths that God illuminates to you. Mysteries are hidden truths and depths in God that you cannot get on the surface, you need to go look for them. Jesus always spoke to the multitudes in parables, to hide the mystery of the Kingdom, from those who could not receive it. God only shares the mysteries of the kingdom to those who can receive it.

*"He answered and said unto them, Because it is given unto you to **know the mysteries of the kingdom of heaven**, but to them it is not given," (Matthew 13:11).*

Jesus revealed to His disciples that the mysteries or hidden truths of the kingdom were only meant for committed disciples. Jesus told us to seek the kingdom first. *"But seek ye first the kingdom of God, and his righteousness; and all these things shall be added unto you,"* (Matthew 6:33) If you do not seek it you will not find it. Many saints do not walk in their kingdom identity because they have not sought it.

Your Identity and Destiny in the Kingdom

A king deals with a kingdom and a priest deals with the church. When you are dealing with Kingdom of God, you must learn His ranks. The Kingdom chart identifies the ranks and destinies, lowest to highest in the Kingdom of God as:

1. Prince
2. King
3. High King or Emperor (Prince or King of Kings)
4. Son of God (Junior god)
5. God Realm (God being with you, inside you, and one with you)
6. God all by Himself

"And from Jesus Christ, who is the faithful witness, and the first begotten of the dead, and the prince of the kings of the earth. **Unto him that loved us, and washed us from our sins in his own blood, And hath made us kings and priests unto God and his Father;** *to him be glory and dominion for ever and ever. Amen,"* (Revelation 1:5-6). Jesus washed your sins in His Blood to make you a king! He made you a king and you must understand the process involved in coming into your kingship. The Lord starts your kingship training by making you a prince. After you master being a prince, He coronates you as a king in the Spirit, and then a high king which means a king of kings or an emperor. Every prince has a principality, every king has a kingdom, and every emperor has an empire.

The Prince is more of a strongman who has a strong garrison, fort, or stronghold, like a city with walls around it. Princes are called strongmen by Jesus (Mark 3:27; Matthew 12:29; Luke 11:21-22). A king rules over many princes in multiple regions, that make up his kingdom and emperors rule kings and their kingdoms. Emperors reign over an empire comprised all the kings and kingdoms of the world.

> Satan's kingdom is set up the same way, it is really an empire because he rules the world as the prince of the world. He has king demons who rule nations and prince demons or principalities that establish strongholds over major regions. The key to subduing demonic rulers is to outrank them. Therefore, princes cast out devils, kings break and cast out princes, and emperors subdue king demons. You can study the ranks beyond these in my Kingdom of God School Series.

The Making of a Prince in God's Kingdom
How to Become a Prince

*"And he said, Thy name shall be called no more Jacob, but Israel: **for as a prince hast thou power** with God and with men, and hast prevailed,"* (Genesis 32:28). Jacob is one of the first princes the Bible mentions. God did not call Jacob a prophet, even though he was a prophet, He called him a prince after he wrestled with an angel all night. Your royal office carries a greater title and rank than your priestly office.

As you see, Jacob was not just a prophet he was a prince. However, hardly anything is taught on the royal side of Jacob or the power and realm of influence you receive when you walk in the power of your Kingdom office. The church is so weak because most major in priestly gifts and anointings rather than learning and majoring in the Kingdom. You can only understand a person's full assignment when you understand their kingdom side. A prince is the son of a king and the heir to the throne. The Bible says, *"Now I say, **That the heir, as long as he is a child, differeth nothing from a servant, though he be lord of all; But is under tutors and governors until the time appointed of the father,"*** (Galatians 4:1-2).

Royal Power of a Prince

A prince is the child of a king and even though he is "lord of all," because of his stage of development, he is delivered over to tutors and governors who bring him up until it is time to be formally inaugurated into kingship. He is a lord but because he is a child he has to serve and go through training to become a king.

You cannot be a prince if you are not the son of a king, therefore, when God makes you a prince, He places you into Sonship. *"... **but ye have received the Spirit of adoption,** whereby we cry, Abba, Father. The Spirit itself beareth witness with our spirit, that **we are the children of God. And if children, then heirs;** heirs of God, and joint-heirs with Christ..."* (Romans 8:15-17). When you were born again, you became a prince, a child of God, and then continue through the process of spiritual maturity, until you become a son of God.

The Father took Jesus through this process during His earthly ministry. ***"And the child grew, and waxed strong in spirit,*** *filled with wisdom: and the grace of God was upon him,"* (Luke 2:40). At the age of 12, Jesus formally started His training as a prince, when He was about His Father's business. As a prince, Jesus increased in favor with God and man.

*"**And Jesus increased in wisdom and stature, and in favour with God and man,**"* (Luke 2:52).

Jesus became a prince in the Spirit during this season of His life. He continued growing and increasing, at the age of 30, He was baptized in the Jordan River by John the Baptist when the Father spoke from Heaven, and formally inaugurated Jesus as His Son! From that time, as a King, Jesus proclaimed the Kingdom of Heaven with power! (Matthew 4:17; Luke 4:14,18). As the firstborn, Jesus mapped out the pathway to your Kingdom destiny! Just as He had to grow you must grow and wax strong as a prince, until you obtain power with God and man as King. Now let us see how Jacob attained the rank of a Prince with God.

Jacob Becomes a Prince in a Wrestling Match

*"And Jacob was left alone; and **there wrestled a man with him until the breaking of the day**. And when he saw that he prevailed not against him, he touched the hollow of his thigh; and the hollow of **Jacob's thigh was out of joint, as he wrestled with him**. And he said, Let me go, for the day breaketh. And he said, I will not let thee go, except thou bless me. And he said unto him, What is thy name? And he said, Jacob. And he said, **Thy name shall be called no more Jacob, but Israel: for as a prince hast thou power with God and with men, and hast prevailed,"***
(Genesis 32:24-28).

This encounter between Jacob and the angel explains what identifies you as a prince with God, not just naturally but spiritually. When you become a spiritual prince, you obtain power with both God and man. You can identity becoming a prince in the spirit, similarly to becoming an apostle, prophet, pastor, or a bishop in the spirit, the first thing that happens is you start winning wrestling matches.

*"**For we wrestle not against flesh and blood,** but against principalities, against powers, against the rulers of the darkness of this world, against spiritual wickedness in high places,"* (Ephesians 6:12).

The Thayer's Greek Definitions describe wrestling as "a contest between two in which each endeavors to throw the other, and which is decided when the victor is able to hold his opponent down with his hand upon his neck." We wrestle against principalities, or territories and strongholds of a prince. You must also understand that princes engage in long, grueling, wrestling matches with principalities, but kings wage and win wars. There are movies where the crown prince of a kingdom is delivered to strong and seasoned warriors to be trained until he becomes a powerful warrior. The young son of the king wrestles and fights men stronger than him because he is learning to be king one day.

Many new Christians have experienced certain kinds of attacks when a being pins them to their bed and they want to cry out to Jesus, but something seems to be stuck, and they can't speak, until they call on Jesus with their spirit, then it breaks. God allows these evil spirits to wrestle you so you can gain strength in the spirit and learn how to exercise your spiritual power. These are very low-ranking demons that seem powerful, because your spirit and power is not strong yet.

> *"For our light affliction, which is but for a moment, worketh for us a far more exceeding and eternal weight of glory,"* (2 Corinthians 4:17).

What you call a major attack, God calls a light affliction that is actually working for your good and giving you more weight in the spirit. Every year, through trials and wrestling matches, you should shift into a higher spiritual weight class. In other words, you should not be binding that spirit that wouldn't let you talk at night anymore, it should be gone!

When I first got saved at seventeen years old, I got attacked by those spirits too. However, I started to fast, pray, and seek God, and when that spirit came back, I broke him immediately and he did not come back because I moved on to greater ranks in the Kingdom where those spirits know not to come. The more you shift in weight, through wrestling, the stronger you become and you prevail over those spirits.

> *"With great wrestlings have **I wrestled with my sister, and I have prevailed...**"* (Genesis 30:8). Wrestling gives you prevailing power in prayer! When you wrestle to the point that you prevail in prayer you come into power with God and power with men as Jacob did. This is called prevailing prayer and it is how you build up strength and become a prince.

Establishing the Stronghold of Peace

The morning time visitation is when you prevail in prayer. To have power with God as a prince, you need to give yourself to this kind of prayer, fasting helps greatly as well. Do you remember when you finished your first long fast and the power of God manifested in your life? You were beginning to prevail spiritually in that moment. During your training to become a prince, you wrestle with principalities and

THE WINGS OF THE MORNING

beings that are stronger than you, and if you keep wrestling until you prevail, you will obtain power with God as a prince.

Jesus came into every kingdom office and rank during His earthly ministry. He is the prince of the principality of peace. ***"And let the peace of God rule in your hearts ..."*** (Colossians 3:15). *"For the kingdom of God is not meat and drink; but righteousness, **and peace,** and joy in the Holy Ghost,"* (Romans 4:17). Peace is part of the Kingdom of God and Jesus is the Prince of that Peace. This peace belongs to you as a child of God, while you are a prince training to become a king.

"Blessed are the peacemakers: for they shall be called the children of God," (Matthew 5:9).

The Peace realm is meant for children, princes and heirs to the throne. As a believer, you must understand the different stages of growth you will go through. You start off as a babe in Christ, then a child of God, and after a process of time, you become a mature son of God. Peacemakers are children of God that is why you must master peace in your princeship. When you are a prince you are still a child, a young son of a king. If you have not prevailed to the point of having peace rule as a stronghold in your life, you have not become a prince yet.

"He that hath no rule over his own spirit is like a city that is broken down, and without walls," (Proverbs 25:28).

As a child of God, if you have not mastered the realm of peace, it is not ruling your heart or spirit, you do not have a stronghold, and you are a city broken down and without walls! When anything and everything upsets you, and you lose your peace, you are not a prince yet. If you panic and lose your peace the moment you hear bad news, you are not a strong man yet, and the devil can come in and steal everything from you. Peace guards your heart and mind and establishes a stronghold in your mind that helps you overcome anything the devil throws at you. Peace is developed in the childhood stage therefore peacemakers are called Children of God.

Prevailing in Prayer as a Prince

*"**Be careful for nothing; but in every thing by prayer and supplication** with thanksgiving let your requests be made known unto God. **And the peace of God, which passeth all understanding, shall keep your hearts and minds** through Christ Jesus, "* (Philippians 4:6-7).

"Keep" in the Greek, means to be a watcher in advance; to mount guard as a sentinel, protect, and keep with a garrison. In other words, when you prevail in prayer and supplication, the peace of God that passes all understanding comes into your life to guard your heart and mind. Your heart and mind become a stronghold, and you have power to cast down imaginations and every high thing that exalts itself against the knowledge of God (2 Corinthians 10:5). To become a stronghold, your heart and mind must be kept garrisoned and guarded by the peace of God, and you are no longer a city broken down and without walls. You come into this as you overcome anxiety and worry and take everything to God in prayer and supplication. Through prayer you prevail and come into the realm of peace. When Jacob wrestled the angel, he prayed! *"Yea, he had power over the angel, and prevailed: he wept, and made supplication unto him,"* (Hosea 12:4).

Being a prince, is power to prevail, advance, and breakthrough obstacles, things, and beings that are hindering your life and destiny. Have you ever felt that you were not prevailing in your ministry or in your life, that you were in some kind of a stalemate and were stuck? If you get up in the morning for a season, you will prevail.

Jesus did not *just* become the Prince of Peace and the Prince of the Kings of the earth, He had to prevail in prayer to obtain the power of a prince with God. He did not have any special privileges because He was the Son of God, He had to go through everything we go through, so He could be our Savior.

*"Who in the days of his flesh, when **he had offered up prayers and supplications with strong crying and tears** unto him that was able to save him from death, and was heard in that he feared; **Though he were a Son, yet learned he obedience by the things which he suffered;** And being made*

> *perfect, he became the author of eternal salvation unto all them that obey him,"* (Hebrews 5:7-9).

Jesus had to offer up prayers and supplications with strong crying and tears, and learn obedience to be perfected. He progressed and prevailed greatly because He understood the mystery and importance of the morning time visitation. Nobody went through as much persecution and trials as Jesus did. The religious leaders were always planning and scheming His death and destruction, and He prevailed through prayer.

The Peace of God that keeps your heart and mind comes through having a strong prayer life. One reason why people cannot be a stronghold in the Kingdom or a prince with God is because they have a weak prayer life. When you establish a strong prayer life, God can bring you to a place where your mind and heart are fixed, settled, and established in the garrison of peace that passes all understanding.

I am a stronghold for God. It does not matter what happens in my life, my heart is fixed, and only the Peace of God brings you to this place. When you become a strong man in the spirit there is a peace that fortifies you. When you attain the rank of a prince you do not have to wrestle or struggle as much anymore, because you are past that stage and once you become a prince you begin to transition into becoming a king where you do not wrestle with principalities and prince demons anymore, because they break immediately at your presence!

CHAPTER 12
Power from God

CHAPTER 12
Power from God

You See God's Power in the Morning

Power from God is when He gives you a measure of anointing, influence, and ability, to perform His will on earth. Power with God is much greater, it is when God brings everything He has, including all of creation to work with you. That is immeasurable and infinite power!

"O God, thou art my God; early will I seek thee: my soul thirsteth for thee, my flesh longeth for thee in a dry and thirsty land, where no water is; ***To see thy power and thy glory,*** *so as I have seen thee in the sanctuary,"*
(Psalm 63:1-2).

You receive God's power and glory in the morning when you get up to meet Him, He gives you a new anointing, a new power, and a new vigor that thickens and gets stronger the more you meet Him in fourth watch prayer.

Jesus came into Kratos power after He continued all night in prayer until the breaking of day. This power flows from the person and glory of the Father over creation, and gives dominion and mastery over the elements of fire, wind, water, earth, time, and space. Jesus demonstrated Kratos power when He walked on water.

THE WINGS OF THE MORNING

*"And when he had sent the multitudes away, **he went up into a mountain apart to pray: and when the evening was come, he was there alone**. But the ship was now in the midst of the sea, tossed with waves: for the wind was contrary. **And in the fourth watch of the night Jesus went unto them, walking on the sea,**"* (Matthew 14:23-25).

The Bible is very detailed about the time Jesus spent praying, specifically that He started in the evening, prayed through the night, and then during the fourth watch, power was released to perform a great marvel. In another account, Jesus spent several days in prayer and it was at daybreak, that He walked in a more powerful dimension of anointing.

*"And it came to pass in those days, that he went out into a mountain to pray, and continued all night in prayer to God. And when it was day, he called unto him his disciples: and of them he chose twelve, whom also he named apostles; And he came down with them, and stood in the plain, and the company of his disciples, and a great multitude of people out of all Judaea and Jerusalem, and from the sea coast of Tyre and Sidon, which came to hear him, and to be healed of their diseases; ... And they that were vexed with unclean spirits: and they were healed. **And the whole multitude sought to touch him: for there went virtue out of him, and healed them all,**"*
(Luke 6:12-13, 17-19).

Jesus already walked in a very strong anointing, laying hands on everyone, but after this time of prayer, people were now touching Him and being made perfectly whole. The power gets richer and thicker on you when you get up early in the morning and pray until the break of day. Power is one of the manifold mercies God releases when He comes down from heaven to visit the earth.

Jesus Received Dominion at His Resurrection

"... the upright shall have dominion over them in the morning,"
(Psalm 49:14).

The word for "dominion" in Hebrew is *rad'ah* and means to tread down, subjugate, have dominion, prevail against, reign, and rule over. This is the same power that Jesus recovered at his death, burial, and resurrection.

> *"... All power is given unto me in heaven and in earth,"* (Matthew 28:18).

The power Jesus was referring to is not a church power, it is a royal Kingdom power that you get when you rise up early in the morning.

> *"But God will redeem my soul from the power of the grave: for he shall receive me"* (Psalm 49:15).

That whole passage (Psalm 49:14-15) is prophetically talking about Jesus. When God redeemed the soul of Jesus from the power of the grave, He came into a greater realm of power than He had before He was crucified. Before His death, Jesus healed the sick, casted out devils, raised the dead, and many more amazing signs and wonders, but when He rose from the dead, He received royal power to sit on the right hand of God. That is royal dominion and the power and glory that Jesus was looking forward to before His death. *"Hereafter shall the Son of man sit on the right hand of the power of God,"* (Luke 22:69). God received Jesus when He rose from the dead, ascended into the third heavens, and was led by the angels into His presence.

> *"The LORD said unto my Lord, Sit thou at my right hand, until I make thine enemies thy footstool,"* (Psalm 110:1).

God gave Jesus the power of the right-hand seat and dominion over His enemies, to *rad' ah* them, or make them His footstool by treading on them with His feet. By paying the price to wake up from sleep, which is a form of death, while it is still dark outside and pray until dawn, you will come into this realm of power where even creation will bow, serve, and obey you!

THE WINGS OF THE MORNING

Virtue is Restored in the Fourth Watch

Do you know that you need virtue in your body to heal the sick? Many people talk negatively and condemn preachers with healing and miracle ministries in general, but especially those who have made mistakes, when the truth is, they have no idea the price that was required of them to walk in that power and anointing. You must understand that ministering to the sick and oppressed is not just about getting behind a pulpit to preach and give a message. When you lay hands and release God's power on His people, virtue or moral excellence, leaves your body. This happened to Jesus when the woman with the issue of blood came to Him for help.

> *"When she had heard of Jesus, came in the press behind, and touched his garment. For she said, If I may touch but his clothes, I shall be whole. And straightway the fountain of her blood was dried up; and she felt in her body that she was healed of that plague.* ***And Jesus, immediately knowing in himself that virtue had gone out of him,*** *turned him about in the press, and said, Who touched my clothes?"* (Mark 5:27-30).

When the woman with the issue of blood touched Jesus and got healed, He felt virtue leaving His body. The word virtue in the gospels is also translated as the miracle-working power of the Holy Spirit, it also means moral excellence. One word for "virtue" in the Greek is *dunamis*, which means "inherent power, power residing in a thing by virtue of its nature, or which a person or thing exerts and puts forth" (Thayer's Greek Definitions G1411). Another word used for "virtue" is *arete* which means "a virtuous course of thought, feeling and action; virtue, moral goodness; any particular moral excellence, as modesty, purity," (Thayer's G703).

> *"And six years thou shalt sow thy land, and shalt gather in the fruits thereof:* ***But the seventh year thou shalt let it rest and lie still;*** *that the poor of thy people may eat: and what they leave the beasts of the field shall eat. In like manner thou shalt deal with thy vineyard, and with thy oliveyard,"*
> (Exodus 23:10-11).

God warned the children of Israel to allow the land to rest in the seventh year so it could regain its virtue, nutrients, and strength. When the land rests, its inherent ability to produce and be fertile is restored, and it can strengthen you. In fact, God exiled Israel from the land so it could rest for 70 years! *"To fulfil the word of the LORD by the mouth of Jeremiah, until the land had enjoyed her sabbaths: for as long as she lay desolate she kept sabbath, to fulfil threescore and ten years,"* (2 Chronicles 36:21). When the land rests it regains its vigor and becomes even more fruitful (Leviticus 26:33-35). In the same way, when you expend virtue in ministry, you need rest because your virtue is your strength.

Virtue is your strength to live right and be virtuous towards God and man. When you minister healing, you are not only giving out power, you also give virtue. Therefore, it does not matter how holy or righteous you have lived for years, when you expend your virtue, you are vulnerable to uncleanliness. Even after Jesus ministered all day, He would go back to His father early in the morning to be refreshed, because He was drained from expending His virtue during the day, *"And the whole multitude sought to touch him:* ***for there went virtue out of him, and healed them all,****"* (Luke 6:19).

Can you imagine how drained Jesus would be after the crusades He had? The virtue leaving His body was not just the anointing and mantle, it was also the inherent strength and ability inside His body. Jesus called me to be the healing shepherd to America, and I learned this by both experience and revelation. Let me show you one way a type of virtue and moral excellence leaves you. I have always been a person who likes to hang up my clothes in a very neat way every time I come home from ministry. I like everything to be neat, clean, and orderly, however, I noticed that after many years in ministry and giving out virtue, which includes one's moral excellence and lifestyle, I got weaker in that area and noticed I didn't do it anymore because my strength and virtue were drained. I am not giving excuses but after many years of expending virtue, I just came home, took off my clothes, dumped them anywhere, and flopped on the bed.

You simply lose the strength or virtue to live like you used to. You keep your virtue by getting up during fourth watch prayer to be with the Lord and receive His new mercies and virtue. At this time, He restores your soul, quickens your body, and renews your strength like an eagle! *"Who satisfieth thy mouth with good things; so that thy youth is renewed like the eagle's,"* (Psalm 103:5).

*"And Jesus said, Somebody hath touched me: **for I perceive that virtue is gone out of me,**"* (Luke 8:46).

If this happened to Jesus, you must understand it will happen to you too. Virtue is always leaving your body and your life when you minister, so having a lifestyle of morning prayer is a must for healing and miracle ministers and ministries. Many ministries have been lost because the minister did not know the importance of being refreshed in the morning time visitation. If you get up in the morning, you will recover, your virtue will be restored, and your healing and miracle ministry will be stronger and more powerful than before!

The Temple Covenant

"To see thy power and thy glory, so as I have seen thee in the sanctuary," (Psalm 63:2).

David specifically mentions that he expects to see God's power and glory in the sanctuary! Do you want to see the power of God hit your church? Rise up early in the morning, go to the church, and meet God when He visits the earth.

*"Even them will I bring to my holy mountain, and make them **joyful in my house of prayer:** their burnt offerings and their sacrifices shall be accepted upon mine altar; **for mine house shall be called an house of prayer for all people,**"* (Isaiah 56:7).

*"And he taught, saying unto them, Is it not written, **My house shall be called of all nations the house of prayer?** but ye have made it a den of thieves,"* (Mark 11:17).

Jesus affirmed what His Father said in the Old Testament, and it stems from a covenant that God made with Solomon when the temple he built for the Lord was dedicated.

*"Moreover concerning **the stranger, which is not of thy people Israel,** but is come from a far country for thy great name's sake, and thy mighty hand, and thy stretched out arm; **if they come and pray in this house; Then hear thou from the heavens, even from thy dwelling place, and do according to all that the stranger calleth to thee for;** that all people of the earth may know thy name, and fear thee, as doth thy people Israel, and may know that this house which I have built is called by thy name,"* (2 Chronicles 6:32-33).

Throughout the prayer of dedication, Solomon talked about how the House of God would be a place for people to come and pray when they are in trouble, at war, when sickness, famine, or pestilence affected them, or when they make mistakes and do wrong things. He also said the stranger will come and pray in the house. From that point, the temple was known as a house of prayer for all nations, and in the New Testament, Jesus kept that covenant! When people ask me why I go to the church and shut in for days on end, I tell them, it is because God made a covenant with our fathers that if we come to the altar in His house, He will hear our prayers and answer them, and He has not changed!

*"And the LORD said unto him, I have heard thy prayer and thy supplication, that thou hast made before me: **I have hallowed this house, which thou hast built, to put my name there** for ever; and **mine eyes and mine heart shall be there perpetually,"*** (1 Kings 9:3).

Most people do not know the revelation of going to God's House to pray or how much more they receive there than in their house. Do you realize that every time you enter the church, God's eyes and heart are set on you? **"... the house of God, which is the church of the living God,** *the pillar and ground of the truth,"* (1 Timothy 3:15). God promised to do this for all who frequent His house.

David said one thing that you can expect to experience in the house of God, and that is that if you rise up early in the morning to go there and pray, you will see God's power and glory. You can have an appearance from God in His House, but because many believers do not study, they do not know the covenants God made with our fathers. We think Jesus simply said, *"My house is called a house of prayer,"* it is much deeper than that! If you cannot get a prayer through to God at home because you are around some heathens and devils, God is saying, if you shut away and fast in the church, He will hear you! His eyes and heart will be set on you, His ears will be attentive to your cry, and He will awaken for you! If there is no peace in your home, know that there is peace in God's!

"Not forsaking the assembling of ourselves together, as the manner of some is; but exhorting one another: and so much the more, as ye see the day approaching," (Hebrews 10:25).

This instruction is even more significant in our day, because the day of the Lord is nearer now than it was then. Therefore, we are not to forsake or neglect meeting with each other in the house of God. Jesus affirmed that when we gather, He appears in our midst! **"For where two or three are gathered together in my name, there am I in the midst of them"** (Matthew 18:20). Jesus was not just making a promise, it is a covenant! Seeing the Lord in the temple is one of the things that belong to your peace in the morning (Psalm 63:1-2).

God promises to answer prayers that are said in His house, even the prayers of strangers, meaning unsaved people. I have seen unbelievers come to the house of God when they were in deep trouble and pray for Him to help them and God answers their prayers, then they go back to their old ways. God does that because He made a covenant over the temple to station His eyes and heart in the House of Prayer continually, for all who enter. If you want to see God, if you want to experience His power on your life, then go to His house early in the morning and do the fourth watch prayer.

Coming into Power with God

When you receive power from God and an anointing to do certain work, you must understand that they are given in stages by the grace and measure of your anointing. Power with God is when He comes with His Power and all of Heaven works directly with you, which is great power indeed! Jacob received this power when the angel said, *"... **as a prince hast thou power with God** and with men, and hast prevailed,"* (Genesis 32:28).

There are a lot of preachers who are greatly gifted and anointed that are doing wonderful things because they have power from God but they do not necessarily have power with God, when He backs them with His power and all of Heaven.

"Many will say to me in that day, Lord, Lord, have we not prophesied in thy name? and in thy name have cast out devils? ***and in thy name done many wonderful works? And then will I profess unto them, I never knew you:*** *depart from me, ye that work iniquity,"* (Matthew 7:22-23).

You can walk in power from God and still be rejected. The preachers in this passage walked in power, but they never got to the stage where they had a real relationship with the Lord. It is when you walk in fellowship with the Lord, where He knows you by name and face that you will have power with God and He works directly with you.

The Lord worked directly with the twelve apostles. *"And they went forth, and preached every where,* ***the Lord working with them, and confirming the word with signs following.*** *Amen,"* (Mark 16:20). They had Jesus with them confirming the spoken word with signs.

God also worked directly with the apostle Paul. ***"And God wrought special miracles by the hands of Paul:*** *So that from his body were brought unto the sick handkerchiefs or aprons, and the diseases departed from them, and the evil spirits went out of them,"* (Acts 19:11-12). God did the miracles Himself through Paul and shook all of Asia with the message of the Kingdom. When God works with you, you shake entire regions!

Jacob came into power with God and with men when he wrestled all night in prayer till daybreak. After that all-night session, we read how a major spiritual transaction took place right at daybreak when Jacob asked the angel to give him a blessing. *"And he said, Let me go, for the day breaketh. And he said, I will not let thee go, except thou bless me. And he said unto him, What is thy name? And he said, Jacob. And he said, Thy name shall be called no more Jacob, but Israel:* **for as a prince hast thou power with God and with men, and hast prevailed,"** (Genesis 32:26-28).

Moses Comes into Marvel Powers with God
The Covenant of Marvels

"Behold, I make a covenant: before all thy people I will do marvels ..."
(Exodus 34:10).

When you come into power with God you enter the realm of marvels, not just miracles. Miracles manifest as a result of God's supernatural intervention in your life and in other people's life. Marvels on the other hand, are God's glory releasing superhuman powers to do acts that are extraordinary and amazing. Marvels are connected to the glory of God that is why God made a covenant of marvels with Moses when He showed him the glory of His back parts on Mount Sinai early in the morning.

"And be ready in the morning, and **come up in the morning unto mount Sinai, and present thyself there to me in the top of the mount,"**
(Exodus 34:2).

"And he said, Behold, I make a covenant: before all thy people I will do marvels, such as have not been done in all the earth, nor in any nation: and all the people among which thou art shall see the work of the LORD: **for it is a terrible thing that I will do with thee,"** (Exodus 34:10).

The covenant that God made with Moses when He showed him His glory on Mount Sinai, is what I call the Covenant of Marvels. Marvels are "terrible things" that manifest the power to cause dread and the fear of God to fall on people, resulting astonishment and awe. Jehovah told Moses that the people *"shall see the work of the LORD."* Marvels are impressive abilities of power that God does with those who have power with Him.

When you walk in marvels, you have the power of supernatural speed like Elijah, who outran the horses and chariots of Ahab the king, or like Moses turned water into blood and split the Red Sea, and like Jesus when He turned water into wine at Cana. You, manifest glory when you walk in marvels! Jesus also walked in marvels when He multiplied bread among thousands, walked on water, and caused a boat to be supernaturally transported. In this last hour, God wants to do marvels through us.

*"For the Father loveth the Son, and sheweth him all things that himself doeth: and **he will shew him greater works than these, that ye may marvel,"***
(John 5:20).

Jesus described marvels as "greater works." ***"... greater works than these shall he do; because I go unto my Father,"*** (John 14:12). We have to work with God the Father to operate prolifically in marvel powers to come into this covenant, you must understand what it means for God to make you a junior god and the importance of coming into full sonship. God could make this covenant of marvels with Moses because He already made him a god! *"And the LORD said unto Moses, See, I have made thee a god to Pharaoh..."* (Exodus 7:1). To get more understanding, you need to get my books, *Sonship in the Kingdom of God* and *Mysteries of the Kingdom of God: The Hidden Secret of Protons*. I teach the process to come into these powers and I outline some of the marvel powers you receive when you get power with God.

God wants to do marvels with you that have never been done or seen on earth! If you want this power with God, start paying the price by getting up early in the morning and presenting yourself before God in prayer.

*"That at that time ye were without Christ, being aliens from the commonwealth of Israel, and **strangers from the covenants of promise,** having no hope, and without God in the world: But now in Christ Jesus ye who sometimes were far off are made nigh by the blood of Christ,"*
(Ephesians 2:12-13).

Manifesting Marvel Powers with God in the 21st Century

We are no longer strangers and aliens from the commonwealth of Israel. By the Blood of Jesus, we have access to all God's covenants of promise. I know this because I am walking in the covenant of marvels. God told me that He gave me what Moses had, and that includes the covenant of marvels. He confirms this covenant by manifesting Himself in the clouds in every region He sends me to.

Bringing God face to face with man is the ultimate marvel power. Moses walked extensively in this power and brought a whole nation out of Egypt to meet with Jehovah on Mount Sinai. He brought God down to the earth for all people to see! It was so marvelous, that the whole earth heard about it!

*"And they will tell it to the inhabitants of this land: **for they have heard that thou LORD art among this people, that thou LORD art seen face to face, and that thy cloud standeth over them,** and that thou goest before them, by day time in a pillar of a cloud, and in a pillar of fire by night,"*
(Numbers 14:14).

God wants to do more in our day! He has entrusted me with the face to face movement and has given me power as a face to face prophet to bring cities and nations to meet with Him! Many cities and nations have seen and experienced the face of God appearing in the clouds as He works with me.

Receiving Power at a "Wist Not" Level

You must understand that power with God will not work if you do not use it or live it. You must do your work and then God will do His. When I teach on fourth watch prayer in churches, the people feel the presence of God, but when they realize they can get power with God, they expect an overwhelming power to hit them and when it does not seem to happen, they are deceived into thinking that nothing really happened when they prayed, but it did! I want to address that thinking by sharing my own morning prayer experiences.

Power from God

For many years of meeting the Lord early in the morning, during fourth watch prayer, mostly sense His beautiful aroma and feel His presence as I fellowship with Him. However, in the evening and at night, when I get behind the pulpit, I feel His power hit and I feel electricity on top of my head and surge powerfully through my body. That is the manifestation of the power I received from God early in the morning. There have been times when months have passed, before I see things that I didn't have before. When Jacob received the blessing of a name change from the angel there was no electricity, and there was no powerful manifestation because God does things at a wist not level. When Moses came down from Mount Sinai after spending 40 days and nights with God, the Bible says, *"... Moses wist not that the skin of his face shone while he talked with him,"* (Exodus 34:29).

When you get this deep with God, it is not uncommon for you to personally not feel any perceptible change, but others will see it, and soon you will begin to realize that something most marvelous is happening with you. In other words, when you get up in the morning and do the fourth watch prayer you receive what I have been sharing with you, but because what you just received was released in the spirit, you don't feel it immediately. The things that belong to you in the morning time visitation are released at a "wist not" level. You do not really realize that you have it until it is time for it to manifest!

Power with God to Heal the Maimed

If power is released in the morning, you must see that there are different manifestations of power that you can ask for. For a number of years, I have spent seasons doing morning time visitation prayer, asking God to restore missing limbs to amputees ever since a young man came and shared a tremendous dream that he had with me. I know that he hears accurately from God, because earlier in my ministry, this same young man prophesied a powerful move that God did through me in Washington State and Chicago, so I knew this dream was significant. In the dream, God showed him that a major revival would break out in Texas. He saw that I did a revival in Texas that grew so big, people started coming from all over the world, and CNN and other news outlets were there. He said apart from people

THE WINGS OF THE MORNING

getting out of wheelchairs something special was happening and causing a stir! Many people with amputated body parts were being healed and the miracles were being filmed by the news media.

To be honest with you, up until now, I have only seen one person with an amputated foot healed in my ministry. This was not a healing it was a miracle! She came forward for prayer, and I asked the Lord to restore her foot, nothing happened at the service, but she came back the next night and God totally restored her foot! I have seen many legs that were shorter than the other one grow out, but amputated legs and hands growing out is a very rare thing in the healing and miracle ministry today. However, it happened in Jesus' ministry and He is bringing it back in our generation!

"And great multitudes came unto him, having with them those that were lame, blind, dumb, maimed, and many others, and cast them down at Jesus' feet; and he healed them: Insomuch that the multitude wondered, when they saw the dumb to speak, **the maimed to be whole,** *the lame to walk, and the blind to see: and they glorified the God of Israel,"* (Matthew 15:30-31).

The maimed are those with missing body parts, and they were made whole in Jesus' ministry. We are supposed to be doing greater works than Jesus did, so we should see this happening in our dispensation. I have been getting up early in the mornings paying the price for this type of power to be restored to us. The Lord started dealing with me and let me know that He wanted to do the same thing with me, because it takes more than having power from Him, these miracles require you to have power *with* God and to get that power, you must pay the price! The Lord told me, *"Just like you had to seek me for two years before I started coming down on earth to work with you by manifesting openly in front of millions of people, you must also pay the price for me to do this with you."*

When you do this kind of prayer you have to be specific. God will show you something He promises to do in your life but you have to ask Him to do it! *"Thus saith the Lord GOD; I will yet for this be enquired of by the house of Israel, to do it for them; I will increase them with men like a flock,"* (Ezekiel 36:37).

Power from God

You need to be specific about what you are asking for. For instance, at one time in my ministry, I was not calling people's first and last names, but I saw how effective I could be if I had that gift of the word of knowledge like Jesus did. For that reason, I started getting up in the mornings asking God to give it to me. I said, *"God give me that level of your power so that people will know that you know the very number of hairs on their heads, including their names. Give me details about your people so I can be effective in ministry. You said in Isaiah 45 to ask of things concerning your sons. Lord, tell me more about your people so I can be a better blessing to them."*

"... I, the LORD, which call thee by thy name, am the God of Israel," (Isaiah 45:3).

God is into calling people by their names to make them believe Him. I prayed for a season asking God to do that for me, and one day it just started happening. The gift dropped on me and at different times in services, I would know someone's name, address, and other details. Over the years, I have come into other manifestations and ranks of power from doing the morning prayer visitation. When you ask, God will grant you your heart's desire. *"Ask, and it shall be given you; seek, and ye shall find; knock, and it shall be opened unto you,"* (Matthew 7:7). The wisdom is to ask at an opportune time.

"Seek ye the LORD while he may be found, call ye upon him while he is near," (Isaiah 55:6).

It is wise to seek and ask the Lord what you want in the morning, when He is physically on earth. If you need power, an anointing, gift, or a certain kind of manifestation, rise to meet Him during fourth watch prayer and God will drop it on you. Many people get frustrated when they are believing and asking God for things, but do not see the manifestation, and they begin blaming Him instead of understanding there are other factors involved in getting prayers answered. One major factor is timing, when you put your requests in at dawn, you will be amazed at how expeditiously things will happen in your life.

Power with Men is Released in the Morning

*"And he said, Thy name shall be called no more Jacob, but Israel: **for as a prince hast thou power with God and with men,** and hast prevailed,"*
(Genesis 32:28).

Power with men is another blessing that belongs to you in the morning visitation. After Jacob wrestled all night in prayer with an angel, he received power with God and men at the breaking of day. When you get power with God, He will also give you power with men. Power with men gives you favor with them to get things done on earth. Power with men will cause them to help you even if they are strangers. *"And strangers shall stand and feed your flocks, and the sons of the alien shall be your plowmen and your vinedressers,"* (Isaiah 61:5). I noticed in my own life and ministry that most of my major connections came through morning prayer.

When you have power with men, God will cause people who tried to stop you turn around and suddenly bless you. I taught this principle to some of my spiritual sons and businessmen on my staff who have multibillion-dollar businesses. I said, *"If you want new accounts to come in to keep expanding your businesses in the millions of dollars, then get up and meet God in the morning to get power with Him and He will also give you power and favor with men."* When they started doing what I told them, they started to get many accounts and found favor with men who were their enemies.

"The king's heart is in the hand of the LORD, as the rivers of water: he turneth it whithersoever he will," (Proverbs 21:1).

When you find power with men and God, He will cause men's hearts to be turned favorably toward you. When Jacob wrestled the angel, he received this and it was manifested when his brother Esau, whom he feared and ran from 20 years earlier, came to him with 400 armed men. It could have been disastrous for Jacob, but this time when Esau met his brother, he was a different man, who had power with God and men. Instead of harming Jacob, Esau made peace with his brother. *"When a man's ways please the LORD, he maketh even his enemies to be at peace with him,"* (Proverbs 16:7).

I can't tell you how many millionaires and billionaires Jesus has visited, to help me get things, because I meet Him in morning prayer. Many times, He appears to them in dreams and tells them to give me money, other times He didn't appear to them at all, because when you do fourth watch prayer, He turns their hearts toward you and gives you favor with them and they give you what you need to do His will.

*"And Jesus increased in wisdom and stature, **and in favour with God and man,**"* (Luke 2:52).

Jesus had power with men because He woke up while it was dark outside, prayed until daybreak, and because He is the bright and morning star, the dayspring that Zechariah prophesied. *"Through the tender mercy of our God; whereby **the dayspring from on high hath visited us,**"* (Luke 1:78). Men and women blessed Jesus throughout His life, from birth until His death!

I remember a season in my life when the Lord told me to give up my mansion and everything I owned, as part of the price, to see Him come down openly in the sight of all men. At this time, I was getting up in the morning seeking the Lord, which is a major part of my relationship with Him. The day my family and I were moving out of the mansion, as the Lord told me, I received a call from a millionaire that I did not know. He told me that he saw our website and had been following the ministry for a year! He also said that the Lord gave him a dream that he would support a ministry that is going to be like Benny Hinn's and that it was about to come on the national scene in a greater way, and to give millions of dollars to this ministry.

That morning as he surfed our website, the Lord whispered to him, *"This is it."* Shortly after he called me, he closed on a 30-milliondollar deal and gave us 3 million dollars! When you do the morning time visitation prayer, God gives you favor with people you do not even know.

Morning Prayer Preserves Favorable Relationships

God gives you favor with men and you come into profitable relationships with them, even the wicked ones who were against you, when you meet Him in the morning. After God gives you power and favor with men, the relationships must be preserved. Therefore, if something is going on that is endangering or jeopardizing them, God will give new mercies to you, in the morning, that will expose what is happening, turn things around, and salvage the relationships.

Every time I go into an extended season of praying early in the morning until daybreak, God reveals snakes aiming for my relationships, through things that are said or misunderstandings that Satan is working on to destroy them. Remember, God gives you favor with men, but He also helps you to keep that favor because Satan likes to divide, break up, and introduce contention and strife to destroy the relationships God gives you.

"A froward man soweth strife: and a whisperer separateth chief friends,"
(Proverbs 16:28).

Satan did that in the garden of Eden when he broke up Adam and Eve's relationship with God. Morning prayer gives you favor with God and man and helps you keep it! I recently found out that a snake was trying to destroy a major relationship I had with someone, but because I was in morning prayer, God revealed what was going on and I was able to deal with the situation, and kill that snake!

Power with Men Draws Multitudes to You

Power with men gives you drawing power and dominion to determine the destinies of millions and billions of souls. Jesus walked in power with men and great multitudes followed Him. *"As thou hast given him **power over all flesh,** that he should give eternal life to as many as thou hast given him,"* (John 17:2). When you pray in the morning, God gives you power over all flesh to give them eternal life!

*"**No man can come to me, except the Father which hath sent me draw him:** and I will raise him up at the last day. It is written in the prophets,*

And they shall be all taught of God. Every man therefore that hath heard, and hath learned of the Father, cometh unto me," (John 6:44-45).

Do you want God to personally teach people who you are in His Kingdom? Evangelists should salivate over the new mercies God releases in the morning. If you want to pack out churches, arenas, coliseums, and stadiums, get up while it is still dark outside and pray until daybreak! Jesus prayed all night until daybreak, and crowds gathered around Him when it was day (Luke 6:12-13, 17).

During a time of intense persecution from false brethren who poisoned a lot of people's minds about me, and crusade crowds were dwindling, the Lord came and told me to do what He did when He spent a number of days praying all night until the breaking of day. He said, *"If you rise up and spend time praying throughout the night until daybreak, the crowds will come back."* I did as Jesus said and the crowds returned greater than ever! A major requirement is that you are vigilant and stay awake throughout this kind of prayer. When I have a major crusade, I spend the whole night praying, and when it is daytime, crowds gather from all over the world to be in these services! A lack of people destroys ministries, but fourth watch prayer will cause God to draw men to you (Proverbs 14:28).

CHAPTER 13
Glory in the Morning

CHAPTER 13
Glory in the Morning

Coming into Your Glory During Fourth Watch

Entering into your glory is another major blessing of the morning time visitation. Jesus entered into His glory after He rose from the dead early in the morning. There is a difference between entering into God's glory and entering into your glory. We know about God's glory but did you know that you also have a glory also? David spoke about his glory when he said, *"Therefore my heart is glad, **and my glory rejoiceth:** my flesh also shall rest in hope,"* (Psalm 16:9). Jesus walked in His glory and the Father's glory.

*"This beginning of miracles did Jesus in Cana of Galilee, **and manifested forth his glory;** and his disciples believed on him,"* (John 2:11).

Jesus manifested His Glory through marvels and miracles when He exercised dominion and mastery over creation and the five elements. Entering your glory happens when God promotes you and raises you up. This happened with Joseph when he said to his brothers, *"And ye shall tell my father of all my glory in Egypt, and of all that ye have seen ..."* (Genesis 45:13). You have a glory that God wants you to come into and when you rise up in the morning to meet God, He will cause your light to come and your glory to begin to manifest. He will promote you and make your name great.

Jesus said, ***"Ought not Christ to have suffered these things, and to enter into his glory?"*** (Luke 24:26). When Jesus rose from the dead early in the morning He came into a greater manifestation of His glory! To talk about your glory is to talk about your destiny, and to fulfill your destiny, you need God to promote you to greatness. Some of you have served the Lord for many years, but you have not entered your glory and you're overdue, if you get up early the wings of the morning will give you speed to catch up in your destiny.

Your glory is whatever treasure God puts inside your earthen vessel, and when He is ready for your debut and to inaugurate you on the day of your showing, He glorifies you. For many years, nobody heard of John the Baptist because God was preparing him in the wilderness, until it was the right time to openly showcase him.

*"And the child grew, and waxed strong in spirit, and was in the deserts **till the day of his shewing unto Israel,"*** (Luke 1:80).

There is a day that God will showcase you openly as well, but it is not something you come into "just because," it takes you meeting God in the morning! God has a spiritual "Broadway" where He debuts and inaugurates you into your glory so He can show the talent, gift, and treasure He placed inside of you, so He can be glorified.

Joseph Comes into His Glory

*"And ye shall tell my father of **all my glory in Egypt**, and of all that ye have seen..."* (Genesis 45:13).

God allows you to enter your glory when you enter your season. As the earth has seasons like sowing and harvesting, winter and summer, you have your own personal seasons as well, and when you come into your season, God ushers you in to your glory. Your glory is your fame and renown, the distinguishing and dominant grace from God that uniquely identifies you. Like Pharaoh said about Joseph,

*"... **Can we find such a one as this is,** a man in whom the Spirit of God is?"* (Genesis 41:38).

Who hits a golf ball like Tiger Woods, serves like Pete Sampras, score goals like Pele of Brazil, hit homeruns like Barry Bonds, or throw touchdown passes like Tom Brady? In the Bible, we would say, who split seas like Moses, had strength like Samson, stopped the sun and moon like Joshua, had wisdom like Solomon, called fire from Heaven like Elijah, healed the sick with his shadow like Peter, or saved the whole world like Jesus? When you come into your glory, people will talk about it! Joseph's glory was the supernatural ability to hear a dream and understand it. God sets you up to enter your glory when you meet with Him in morning time prayer and visitation.

When you come into your glory you walk in things that nobody else can manifest like you. Pharaoh said to Joseph, *"... there is none so discreet and wise as thou art,"* (Genesis 41:39). When I was in my thirteenth year of ministry, God started bringing me into my glory and was doing amazing things with me, because He released greater glory on my life. People began talking about the miraculous things happening during my crusades, and I was concerned because I never wanted to steal God's glory, I wanted to be sure I was doing His ministry, not my own. When I expressed my concerns in prayer to the Lord, He responded with these amazing words, *"I want to see what you will do with your glory before I allow you to walk in my glory."* That revelation crystallized my understanding of what walking in your own glory is compared to walking in God's glory.

If you are faithful in walking in your glory, He will promote you into His glory. When God comes on earth in the fourth watch and you meet Him at that time, He will promote you into your glory. God has a bright future for you. Endure every affliction and suffering, whether it is being ostracized, talked about, or persecuted, take it and move on with God, because that is how you construct the weight for the glory that God desires to put on you. Remember, as Jesus said, suffering is the price for glory. *"Ought not Christ to have suffered these things, and to enter into his glory?"* (Luke 24:26).

You See God's Glory in the Morning

"O God, thou art my God; early will I seek thee ... To see thy power **and** *thy glory, so as I have seen thee in the sanctuary,"* (Psalm 63:1-2).

THE WINGS OF THE MORNING

God shows you His glory when you seek Him early in the morning as David did. When God talks about showing His glory, He comes on earth to show Himself openly before everyone, like He did with Moses and as He is with me. That is beholding His glory, the Father in person! Moses came into this realm when he asked to see God's glory. ***"And he said, I beseech thee, shew me thy glory,"*** (Exodus 33:18). When Moses asked to see God's glory, he could see the glory back parts (Exodus 34:1-10).

If you want to see God's glory you must get up and meet Him in the morning when He visits the earth, because when He passes by in the morning time visitation, you have the opportunity to see Him face to face!

> *"And he said, **I beseech thee, shew me thy glory**. And he said, I will make all my goodness pass before thee, and I will proclaim the name of the LORD before thee; and will be gracious to whom I will be gracious, and will shew mercy on whom I will shew mercy. And he said, Thou canst not see my face: for there shall no man see me, and live. And the LORD said, Behold, there is a place by me, and thou shalt stand upon a rock: **And it shall come to pass, while my glory passeth by, that I will put thee in a clift of the rock, and will cover thee with my hand while I pass by: And I will take away mine hand, and thou shalt see my back parts:** but my face shall not be seen,"*
> (Exodus 33:18-23).

In this glorious scripture, Moses asks to see the glory of God. The interesting thing is that Moses was already speaking to God face to face. *"And the LORD spake unto Moses face to face, as a man speaketh unto his friend,"* (Exodus 33:11). If God was speaking to Moses face to face, why did he ask to see the glory of God? Up until this point, Moses was seeing the similitude or the form of God, when He came in a cloud that formed around Him, outlining His image, but Moses wanted more! He wanted to see God in person! Most believers today would be satisfied seeing only a similitude. I want more! If you want more too, you should value morning time prayer.

Most preachers take the scripture that you cannot see God and live out of context and teach it wrong. If it was true, why would God tell us multiple times to seek His face? When He said that to Moses it was because our sin condition prevented us from seeing His face, not because there is death in His face! *"But your iniquities have separated between you and your God, **and your sins have hid his face from you...**"* (Isaiah 59:2). It was our sins that hid His face from us. Therefore, God sent Jesus to the earth to die for us, redeem us from our sins, and to reconcile us back to Him.

"To wit, that God was in Christ, reconciling the world unto himself..." (2 Corinthians 5:19).

When Jesus died on the cross, the veil was removed and nothing hinders us from having face to face contact with the Father. You can see God and live! *"Seek the LORD, and his strength: **seek his face evermore,**"* (Psalm 105:4). I have seen the Father Face to Face and I am alive because He is not the God of the dead, He is the God of the living! If Moses saw the back parts of God before Jesus reconciled us to the Father, Isaiah saw God high and lifted up, and Daniel saw the head and white hair of God, then what do we have since Jesus reconciled us back to God the Father? We have much more of God than the saints of old ever did!

God told Moses, **"Behold there is a place by me and thou shall stand upon a rock"** That means God was physically on earth with Moses. He goes on to say, **"And it shall come to pass, while my glory passeth by, that I will put thee in a clift of the rock..."** (Exodus 33:21-22). Even though God was physically on earth with Moses, He did not reveal Himself. God said, "it shall come to pass." Most people read Exodus 33 and think the Lord really appeared to him then, but the appearance Moses was asking for didn't happen until Exodus 34.

*"And the LORD said unto Moses, Hew thee two tables of stone like unto the first: and I will write upon these tables the words that were in the first tables, which thou brakest. **And be ready in the morning, and come up in the morning unto mount Sinai, and present thyself there to me in the top of the mount** ... and Moses rose up early in the morning, and went up unto mount Sinai, as the LORD had commanded him, and took in his hand the*

two tables of stone. And the LORD descended in the cloud, and stood with him there, and proclaimed the name of the LORD," (Exodus 34:1-2, 4-5).

"Morning" in the Hebrew is *boqer*, means "dawn, as the break of day." God basically told Moses, *"If you want to see me pass by, be ready at dawn, at the break of day!"* In Exodus 33, Moses was communing with the Lord at noon or in the evening, since He asked Moses to be ready in the morning, proving again that God visits the earth at the breaking of day.

"... and Moses rose up early in the morning, *and went up unto mount Sinai, as the LORD had commanded him,"* (Exodus 34:4). "Early" in Hebrew *shakam* means to load up or to start early in the morning. Moses did not just go up Mount Sinai at dawn, he set out and climbed the mountain early in the morning before daybreak, and was already stationed on the mount, before God descended!

"And the LORD descended in the cloud, and stood with him there, *and proclaimed the name of the LORD,"* (Exodus 34:5).

David Sought God's Glory During Fourth Watch

King David understood this mystery, he knew he could see God early in the morning, because that is when He visits the earth. David was not only a man after God's heart, he pursued His desires, and could hardly wait to wake up early with an intense and insatiable desire to be intimate with God morning by morning.

"O God, thou art my God; **early will I seek thee:** *my soul thirsteth for thee, my flesh longeth for thee in a dry and thirsty land, where no water is;* **To see thy power and thy glory, so as I have seen thee in the sanctuary,"*
(Psalm 63:1-2).

The phrase **"early will I seek thee"** is *shachar* in Hebrew and means "to dawn, to be early at any task, to search for, to seek diligently in the morning." King David would get off his bed very early in the morning and rush to the tent he erected for the ark of God, like a deer panting for water in the wilderness. He was not only seeking the presence of God he was seeking the person of God! *"To see thy power* *and thy glory, **so as I have seen thee in the sanctuary.***" Like Moses, David had the same desire to see the glory of God. He went to the tabernacle looking for God, to seek His person, and His face.

*"... my heart said unto thee, **Thy face, LORD, will I seek,**"* (Psalm 27:8).

*"Seek the LORD, and his strength: **seek his face evermore,**"* (Psalm 105:4).

God's Glory vs Your Glory

God allowed me to come into my glory, the renown, gifts, and talents that He put on my life, and allowed the fame of my name to spread abroad in the first 20 years of my walk with Him through miracle crusades and services I held all over America and in many nations of the world. If I did not know better, I would have only come out of the 20-year process with my glory, but the Father said to me, *"I want to see what you will do with your glory before I allow you to walk in my glory."*

God gives you your glory to test your motives and intentions, to see if after you walk in your glory, will you still be hungry and thirsty for His? When God first sent Moses to Pharaoh, Moses walked in great glory because God made him a god to Pharaoh. Moses did great exploits with the glory that God allowed to come on his life. He turned water into blood, brought swarms of flies, locusts, hail, and fire on the land of Egypt, and split the Red Sea, and in the wilderness, he preserved the children of Israel by bringing manna down from heaven and causing water to flow out of rocks. The glory Moses walked in was so amazing, but at Mount Sinai, Moses cried out to God, *"I beseech thee, shew me thy glory,"* (Exodus 33:18). When God brings you into your own glory, you must begin to seek His glory as Moses did.

God did not just meet Moses in the morning and go back up to Heaven, He stayed on the mount with Moses for 40 days and nights! God's pattern is to come on earth every morning and go back to Heaven, but if He finds a face to face friend on the earth, He will call him up into a place to be alone with Him and come from Heaven and be with that person every day, all day, for a season! When Moses came down from the mountain after 40 days his face was shining, because he accessed God's glory meeting Him during early morning visitation. Moses' direct contact with God caused Him to do the incredible miracles he did.

> *"... Behold, I make a covenant: **before all thy people I will do marvels**, such as have not been done in all the earth, nor in any nation: and all the people among which thou art shall see the work of the LORD: **for it is a terrible thing that I will do with thee,**"* (Exodus 34:10).

Meeting God in the morning time visitation brings you into God's glory, however, many Christians and major leaders in the Body of Christ are getting drunk on their own glory and they do not seek God's. They never say, *"God I want to see Your Glory."* God has made their name great and made them famous all over the earth, they think that is the ultimate, and have no clue that there is so much more if they could see past themselves and come into God's glory.

When you come into your own glory and do not go after God's, you become corrupt like Satan. God is looking for His people to go beyond their glory and ask for His! Walking in God's glory is infinitely greater than walking in your own glory, and it is when you will turn the world upside down!

Manifesting God's Glory as Sons

In my own ministry, I have not propelled my glory or my ministry, because only God's glory changes the world (Isaiah 60:1-3).

> *"And the LORD said, Behold, there is a place by me, and thou shalt stand upon a rock: And it shall come to pass, **while my glory passeth by, that I will put thee in a clift of the rock, and will cover thee with my hand while I pass by:** And I will take away mine hand, and thou shalt see my back parts: but my face shall not be seen,"* (Exodus 33:21-23).

When you talk about God's glory, you are talking about His person, not just His presence. *"Who being the brightness of his glory, and the express image of his person..."* (Hebrews 1:3). When a lot of preachers talk about glory, they are usually referring to an anointing, and that is inaccurate.

God's glory is the foundation of my ministry, and what the Face to Face Movement is all about. This movement prepares atmospheres to receive the persons of God and His Son on earth! Breaking through to this realm in ministry, is no longer about a gift or an anointing manifesting, it is God's government! To walk in God's glory, you must first walk in Sonship, it is the rank in God's Kingdom that demonstrates His glory consistently!

*"For I reckon that the sufferings of this present time are not worthy to be compared with **the glory which shall be revealed in us.** For the earnest expectation of the creature **waiteth for the manifestation of the sons of God,"*** (Romans 8:18-19).

For the people of God to begin walking in glory, they must mature spiritually. *"... no more children, tossed to and fro, and carried about with every wind of doctrine, by the sleight of men, and cunning craftiness, whereby they lie in wait to deceive,"* (Ephesians 4:14). God does not want you to be stuck at the childhood stage of development, but sadly, most of His people are. After twenty years of following hard after God, He brought me into His glory and started coming down visibly in the clouds, manifesting Himself face to face all over America, confirming that He is working with me. Sons who are fully mature display God's glory.

To make speed and progress in your spiritual maturity you must meet God when He comes on earth. *"For a thousand years in thy sight are but as yesterday when it is past, **and as a watch in the night,"*** (Psalm 90:4). A watch in the night is like a thousand years to God and the fourth watch is the time that Jehovah comes from Heaven to earth to visit mankind. When you meet Him at that time, you accelerate at light speed toward your destiny!

Spiritual maturity is not about how long you've been in ministry, it is when you grow out of being a babe in Christ and a child of God and become a son of God. The 18 to 20-year process matures and brings you into Sonship. When you fulfill this process, you will come into God's glory and He will allow it to be seen on you, you will begin to walk in God's image and likeness, and His molecular structure is activated within you to act, talk, and walk in marvels like God.

Many think they are only called to the fivefold ministry as apostles, prophets, and so on, but you are so much more than that, your original destiny is to be the express image of God's glory on earth and to manifest signs and wonders like Jesus did. When you come into Sonship, you not only manifest your glory, you manifest God's!

You Need Meekness to Manifest God's Glory

When you manifest God's glory He will come down on earth and work with you directly. But for that to happen you must first develop meekness. When I was about to complete the 20-year process Jesus appeared to me and said, *"David, My Father is about to start coming down on earth to work with you like He worked with me and Moses, but He requires you to pay the price, because He does not work on earth with every man like that. You have developed humility and now you must develop meekness if you want Him to come down on earth."* Then Jesus said to me, *"Do you want to know why God came down on earth with Moses and used him the way He did? It was because he was the meekest man on earth!"*

This was when I finally understood the secret to Moses' unprecedented ministry. He paid the price of meekness above every other man on earth! The Bible says, **"Now the man Moses was very meek, above all the men** *which were upon the face of the earth,"* (Numbers 12:3). Moses' meekness was why God could work through him so powerfully, and why his ministry outweighed everyone else's in the Old Testament. When I developed meekness, I made the required transaction for God to come on earth like He did with Moses, because God values meekness very highly.

"But let it be the hidden man of the heart, in that which is not corruptible, even the ornament of a **meek and quiet spirit,** *which is in the sight of God of great price,"* (1 Peter 3:4).

Glory in the Morning

A heart of meekness is of great price to God! The Greek word for "meekness" is *praus* which means "mild and gentle." Meekness is the composure of character that keeps you from retaliating and causes you to be mild-mannered and gentle with others. God wants us to walk in meekness because this character is connected to salvation and restoration. *"... he will beautify the meek with salvation,"* (Psalm 149:4).

Many people do not have this character and it needs to be developed! Jesus saved me from a wild gangster lifestyle, in fact, I was in a shootout the night that He appeared to me in a dream and saved me face to face! I was not meek and needed to be changed. Like Jacob, I needed a transformation in my character. Your character and nature are transformed in the early morning visitation and that is when you should ask for and develop meekness! The Bible says, *"The meek will he guide in judgment: and the meek will he teach his way,"* (Psalm 25:9). When God wakes you morning by morning, and gives you the ear of the learned, He is developing meekness in your character!

Jesus said, *"Blessed are the meek: for they shall inherit the earth,"* (Matthew 5:5). If you want God to do anything with you on the earth you must develop meekness. God came to earth and openly manifested Himself, face to face, because He found a meek man that He could work with (Exodus 19:9; Num 14:14). Jesus also had God openly working with Him on earth, in the sight of all, because He developed meekness. He said, *"... I am meek and lowly in heart,"* (Matthew 11:29). It takes humility to walk with God in intimacy and fellowship, but it takes meekness to work with Him!

I have the Face to Face Movement on my life now because I paid the price and developed meekness. Because I developed the heart of Jesus, He rewarded and granted me the amazing manifestation of His glory, by appearing to people in dreams and in the physical realm after they read *Face to Face Appearances from Jesus: The Ultimate Intimacy*, the book that the Lord commissioned me to write, and not only is Jesus appearing but God has been appearing face to face in thick clouds like He did with Moses.

I want to walk and work with God.

Jesus brought the Father down on earth because He is meek and lowly in heart. Not only did He bring God on earth in the sight of men, the Father was also inside of Jesus manifesting face to face with man! *"And without controversy great is the mystery of godliness: God was manifest in the flesh..."* (1 Timothy 3:16). **"... he that hath seen me hath seen the Father,"** (John 14:9).

It is time for you to manifest God's glory on the earth too, not just your own. Rise early in the morning to meet with God and you will have His power and glory like David did (Psalm 63:1-2). When Moses asked to see God's glory Jehovah instructed him to come up Mount Sinai early in the morning. Just as plants grow supernaturally when God is on earth during the fourth watch, you will grow, spring up, and flourish spiritually until you become a son of God! Even if you have lost time in your spiritual growth you can catch up with the wings of the morning and when you mature you will manifest God's glory in the earth.

CHAPTER 14
History and Mysteries of Fourth Watch Prayer

CHAPTER 14
History and Mysteries of Fourth Watch Prayer

God Commands the Morning When He Visits the Earth

I want to share another amazing thing God does every morning when He visits the earth, He commands the morning. I know there are many books and teachings on commanding the morning, and yes when God is in us, we can do certain things, but you will see that commanding the morning is really an act and work of God. This is something He does when He comes on the earth, not us.

"Hast thou commanded the morning since thy days; and caused the dayspring to know his place," (Job 38:12).

God rebuked Job after he questioned Him about the trial he was going through and He asked Job many questions, including if He has ever commanded the morning since he was born, or if he could make the dayspring know his place. God is basically saying to Job, ***"Ever since the beginning of creation I have commanded the morning every single day."*** We think when God said, "Let there be light" and light came, and when He created all the luminary bodies, that He only commanded it once. That is not true, it was not a one-time command, God commands them every morning.

Ever since the world began, God has come on earth to command the mornings, and it is also why the sun rises at different times during different seasons. Every time you check the weather you will notice that the sun rises at a different time almost every day, it never rises at the same time in every season or year. For that reason, God asked Job if he has ever commanded the day.

God Makes the Dayspring Know His Place

God is showing Job that the dayspring dawns at different times in every season and at different times each year. The question is, who is the one commanding the sun to rise, the dawn to come, and when. Who is the one determining when the dawn comes and when the day breaks? God is the one commanding the morning and the dayspring every day. He speaks to the light just like He did at the beginning when He said, "Let there be light," that was projected into multiple generations, and has not stopped! God is still commanding the morning, sun, moon, and stars as He did when He commanded them to be set in the heavens to give light on earth and to determine days, years, signs, and seasons.

As the governor of the earth, God is still ordering things to take place. Even though God has given man the free will to do things, even evil things, and to get things out of order, He is still on earth and in control. *"... he is a great King over all the earth,"* (Psalm 47:2). He commands the morning, the dayspring, and the dawn every morning. It is not the meteorologists who determine when the sun comes up in the morning, they can discern what time the sun rises with their instruments, but they cannot creatively determine when it does.

If you rise in the morning, He will command how your day goes, and give new mercies that will make your day go well. Commanding the morning is also part of God creating order on earth, and in your day. Your steps will be established by the Lord, you will prosper, and this belongs to you every morning when God visits the earth!

Discernment to Choose a Staff
Jesus Chooses His 12 Disciples After Morning Prayer

"And it came to pass in those days, that he went out into a mountain to pray, and continued all night in prayer to God. ***And when it was day, he***

called unto him his disciples: and of them he chose twelve, whom also he named apostles," (Luke 6:12-13).

Discernment to choose a staff of disciples is very important in every ministry. Too many leaders end up choosing the wrong people who bring division, strife, and contention into their ministry, because they do not have discernment. Many ministers have had assistants and staff members walk off with half of their church or ministry. Jesus did not leave the choice of His disciples to chance He had several men and women following and needed discernment to choose 12 of them.

Discernment is the ability to choose between right and wrong, and some have it and some do not. *"But strong meat belongeth to them that are of full age, even those who **by reason of use have their senses exercised to discern both good and evil,**"* (Hebrews 5:14). There has to be a maturity in your development for you to be able to make the right choice, and it takes practice and experience. They say, "practice makes one perfect," but if you get up early in the morning and pray until daybreak, God will help you and give you discernment without the need to rely on a trial and error system. You can get it right every time!

*"I have manifested thy name unto the men which thou gavest me out of the world: **thine they were, and thou gavest them me;** and they have kept thy word,"* (John 17:6).

Jesus acknowledged that His disciples were given to Him by the Father. This belongs to your peace in the morning because God gives you the ability to choose a staff and the knowledge of how each person will turn out. You will know who will betray you and who will be loyal to you. Jesus knew all this at the time He chose His disciples!

Jesus Knew Who Would Betray Him

Jesus had a huge ruckus with His disciples when they argued with Him after He multiplied the bread among the thousands and claimed to be the Living Bread that came down from Heaven and when Jesus spoke to them about eating His Body and drinking His Blood. This conversation threw the disciples off! However, Jesus is a rock of offense and He will say things that offend your mind, to reveal your heart.

> *"But there are some of you that believe not. **For Jesus knew from the beginning who they were that believed not, and who should betray him.** And he said, **Therefore said I unto you, that no man can come unto me, except it were given unto him of my Father.** From that time many of his disciples went back, and walked no more with him,"* (John 6:64-66).

Jesus knew from the beginning who would be loyal and who would betray Him! How did he know that? The answers came during morning time visitation prayer! He chose the disciples after many days of praying all night. Knowing in advance the destiny and end of your disciples helps you help you preserve them. For example, Jesus knew when Satan was attacking His disciples.

> *"And the Lord said, Simon, **Simon, behold, Satan hath desired to have you,** that he may sift you as wheat: **But I have prayed for thee, that thy faith fail not:** and when thou art converted, strengthen thy brethren,"*
> (Luke 22:31-32).

When God visits the earth in the morning, if you are up to meet Him, He will talk to you about your staff and show you who to put in leadership positions. Jesus knew by discernment that Peter was going to be the leader of the 12 apostles, so even when he saw that Peter would deny Him three times, He did not cut him off. Instead, Jesus interceded for him and walked in omega power to preserve Peter's destiny! After Jesus' resurrection, He appeared to and restored Peter after he denied Him, because He knew Peter's destiny from the beginning when He prayed.

Over the years and with every staff I have had, God has always shown me beforehand when someone on my staff is about to betray, which gives me time to warn them and to help them overcome the attack Satan is strategizing against them. The ones who listen to my warnings and instructions get preserved and those who don't fall out. Knowing all this in advance also prepares your heart so you do not get bitter and discouraged. Jesus knew that Judas would betray Him but He kept the right spirit with him.

> *"Jesus answered them,* ***Have not I chosen you twelve, and one of you is a devil? He spake of Judas Iscariot the son of Simon:*** *for he it was that should betray him, being one of the twelve,"* (John 6:70-71).

Jesus knew that Judas was a devil and would betray Him and His love for Judas never wavered! Jesus loved Judas beyond what He knew about him. It is important to notice, Jesus never took Judas along with Him to the Mount of Transfiguration to pray or on any sensitive missions. When Jesus prayed for the 12-year-old girl, He took Peter, James, and John, His inner circle disciples. Having discernment about your staff is so important. Getting up at 3 a.m. and praying until the breaking of day preserves your ministry and helps you avoid disastrous church and ministry splits.

Mysteries of Fourth Watch Prayer

I want to share with you some mysteries of the morning time visitation prayer so you can get the most out of this time with God. Over the years, I have discovered other mysteries of early morning time visitation that make this prayer more effective. You must understand, it is not enough to get up in the fourth watch to pray, you must also know what to do before and during that time to receive the fulness and depth of the visitation. These are deep truths that will bless everyone who wants to take the revelation of fourth watch prayer to the next level and come into all that God has for them.

You Must Get Up Long Before Daybreak

For this prayer to be effective, the first key is that you must be up long before dawn. *"If thou wouldest seek unto God betimes, and make thy supplication to the Almighty,"* (Job 8:5). For example, Jacob started wrestling the angel while it was dark outside (Genesis 32:22-24). If it

THE WINGS OF THE MORNING

is light outside when you wake up, you missed the visitation. Remember, God is on a time schedule.

Jesus the Bright and Morning Star understood this mystery. *"And in the morning, rising up a great while before day, he went out, and departed into a solitary place, and there prayed,"* (Mark 1:35). Jesus started His morning prayer "a great while before day." The Young Literal Translation more accurately depicts this scripture, ***"And very early, it being yet night,*** *having risen, he went forth, and went away to a desert place, and was there praying."* (Mark 1:35). It must be dark outside when you start praying.

It is beautiful to pray in the morning daylight, but it is not the fourth watch prayer. Remember, even if you rise up two hours before sunrise and pray, you will still make contact. However, if you want full contact, you need to start at 3 a.m. The visitation starts at 3a.m., and to get the full benefit, you cannot be in the flesh. You must be dead to the flesh, to be spiritually connected and engaged, when God visits the earth. Paul said, *"...I die daily,"* (1 Corinthians 15:31). Death to the flesh happens when we get in prayer. In my own experience, I have noticed I get the greatest rewards of the morning time visitation when I get up at 12 and pray for three hours and then when the actual visitation starts at 3 a.m. it is just straight fellowship and hearing the voice of God.

When you get up and start praying at 3 a.m. it takes time for you to die to the flesh. It takes about an hour to die to the flesh and then for the next two hours you are tuned in and engaged spiritually. If you want a longer sustaining fellowship with the Lord when He comes, get up at 12 so you can die to the flesh as you labor in prayer till 3 a.m. Like Jesus, you need to get up a great while before day, while it is still night and start praying to be ready and in place, before the visitation starts to receive the full benefits of the morning time visitation.

This is a Seasonal Type of Prayer

I must emphasize that fourth watch prayer is not an everyday kind of prayer. You rise and meet God when He visits the earth for certain seasons as the Lord leads you because each time you rise up in the night and pray until daybreak you are covering many days in the spirit, depending on your spiritual growth. God knows it is hard on your body, and that is why He rewards you for doing it.

Someone on my staff had a dream and God revealed that He covers 12 days every time she gets up and prays in the fourth watch! Your spiritual maturity determines how many days are covered when you meet God in the fourth watch. If you use this dream as a blue print, you can cover a whole year in 30 days of early morning prayer. If it takes you longer to get out of the flesh in the fourth watch, you will clearly make less progress than someone who rises up early enough to die to the flesh sooner and is fully sober and in the spirit before the visitation starts.

A Mature Son Covers 1000 Years in One Fourth Watch

There is a point you can get in the spirit when you can cover 1000 years in just one fourth watch prayer session. This happens when you finish the 20-year process and become a full-grown son of God. Jesus provided eternal redemption for all those who believe in Him through morning prayer. *"For a thousand years in thy sight are but as yesterday when it is past, and as a watch in the night,"* (Psalm 90:4).

When I finished my 20-year process, Jesus appeared to me and told me He was going to take me to meet the Father, but before He took me on this trip to Heaven He said, *"When you meet My Father, your brain will come back to life and you will be able to do incredible things."* When I stood before the Father in Heaven He said, *"David, the first thing I do is give you a brain resurrection."* Then the Father gave me the most amazing teaching I had ever heard in my life.

"David, Adam had 100% capacity of his brain when I created him. Scientists are not lying when they say that you only use of 8-10% of your brain

capacity. The rest of your brain died at the fall" That is why at a certain stage of your spiritual growth Jesus brings you to the Father so He will resurrect your brain and you will begin to operate at 100% full brain capacity. Jesus told us that He is the way to the Father (John 14:6) and He is the one who reveals the Father (Matthew 11:27). When you reach the stage of development where Jesus brings you to the Father for a brain resurrection, that is being fully reconciled to the Father! Many believers never get to this stage of Sonship, because the church has been dwarfed by the fivefold ministry and many in the Body of Christ are stuck at the childhood stage of their spiritual growth. Preachers do not teach on sonship because they do not know it. After spending almost 9 months shut away in a church in Port Huron, Michigan in 2009, the Lord Jesus walked through a wall and physically appeared to me in the room and revealed this to me. I share more on this in my book, *Sonship in The Kingdom of God."*

When you work directly with the Father in this manner, just one day with Him, is like a thousand years. *"...one day is with the Lord as a thousand years, and a thousand years as one day,"* (2 Peter 3:8). I pray that you get to Sonship and experience the Father in His fulness and do greater things than what Moses and the other saints of old did, every time He comes on the earth with you.

How God Applies the Years You Cover in Prayer

> *"That Christ may dwell in your hearts by faith; that ye, being rooted and grounded in love, May be able to comprehend with all saints **what is the breadth, and length, and depth, and height,"*** (Ephesians 3:17-18).

In your spiritual development, you are supposed to grow in every dimensions of Christ: breadth, length, depth, and height. God expects you to grow in all these areas. *"And the remnant that is escaped of the house of Judah shall again take **root downward, and bear fruit upward,"*** (Isaiah 37:31). As an oak of righteousness, you first take root downward and then bear fruit upward. When you can cover years, in just days of fourth watch prayer, you grow backward, forward, deep, and high.

If you do the opposite, and spend every day in unbelief, doubt, and disobedience, you will be set back years. God judged Israel for believing an evil report about the land He promised them, and sentenced them to wander in the wilderness for 40 years, a year for each day the spies spent surveying the land! *"And your children shall wander in the wilderness forty years, and bear your whoredoms, until your carcases be wasted in the wilderness. After the number of the days in which ye searched the land, even forty days, each day for a year, shall ye bear your iniquities, even forty years, and ye shall know my breach of promise,"* (Numbers 14:33-34). God judged them with 40 years of wandering for their 40 days of unbelief. You must understand this concept. *"And I will restore to you the years that the locust hath eaten...."* (Joel 2:25). Fourth watch prayer redeems time lost in the past, and even time in the future that threaten to end your life prematurely.

God does not apply every year you cover in fourth watch prayer into the future or forward. He wants you to be balanced, so you do not go too far ahead and destroy yourself, because you do not have enough foundation built up to last. He applies those years backward or deep into your roots or foundations, so He can fulfill and complete you. You may be spending seasons in fourth watch prayer and nothing seems to be happening, but what is happening is that you are taking root downward and God is strengthening your foundation, so you can be stable, steadfast, and sure in the years of progress, promotion, and exaltation that are coming in your life. Without this, you will crash, burn, and destroy your destiny. God always takes me backwards before shooting me forward.

Ever since the Lord revealed these mysteries of fourth watch prayer to me, I have covered many years, generations, and ages in the spirit which is how I have caught up to the ancient glories and powers of the fathers. At the time this book was written, I caught up to Enoch, when the Father came down and started walking with me in a church where I shut-away with Him. He said, *"David, you have now come into the walk like Enoch had with me. Every day I will come down on earth and walk with you."* The Father comes down physically to walk with me as He did with Enoch, because I paid the price and entered into that realm. Remember, the more years you cover in morning prayer, the more inheritances of the Fathers you come into.

I received the inheritance of Moses in 2006, the ancient civilizations in 2009 during 9 months of consecration and shut-in, because of morning prayer and God applied the years I was covering in prayer backward. I know some of you will find this hard to believe, but it is true, and it is scriptural. I share all this to stir your heart and spirit to pray in the fourth watch! How else do you think Moses was able to write his five books describing in great detail all that happened to the patriarchs before and after the flood? How was he able to foretell all that would happen to Israel in the last chapters of Deuteronomy? He journeyed to the past and covered years that God applied to the past as he spent time before God in the glory and before He died, God took him on a spiritual journey into the future to see all that Israel would go through. A day with the Lord is indeed like a thousand years! When you do fourth watch prayer frequently, your development in the spirit will be complete and more sustained. You will be built to last, and if you happen to cover more years than you can fulfill in this age then guess what, it will be accounted for your favor in the ages and generations to come in eternity. This all belongs to your peace in the morning!

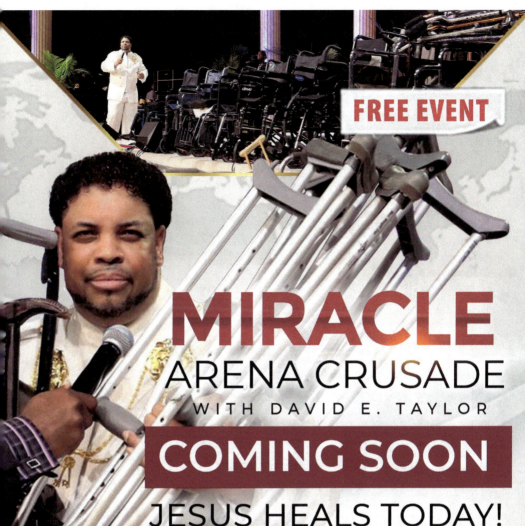

MIRACLE
ARENA CRUSADE
WITH DAVID E. TAYLOR

FREE EVENT

COMING SOON

JESUS HEALS TODAY!
Amway Center In Orlando, FL

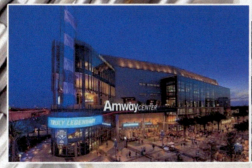

FOR FREE REGISTRATION VISIT
JOSHUAMEDIAMINISTRIES.ORG

OR CALL TO REGISTER
1.877.843.4567

FACE-TO-FACE

"I Will Come To You!" ~ Jesus (John 14:18)

Because of this book, millions around the world are experiencing intimacy in a deeper and whole new and fresh way, through Face to Face Appearances with Jesus

Order Your Copy Today!

And Experience Deeper Intimacy With Christ! Call 1.877.THE GLORY or go online to Joshuamediaministries.org

Order Today!

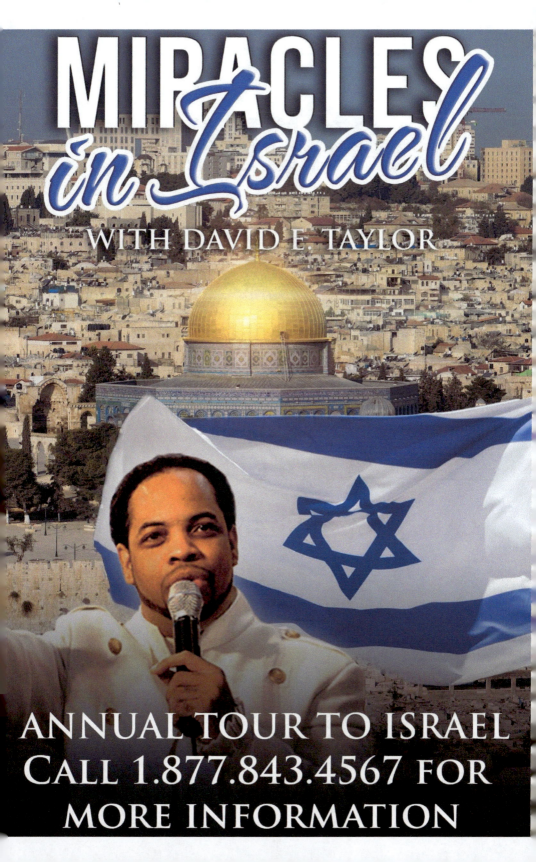

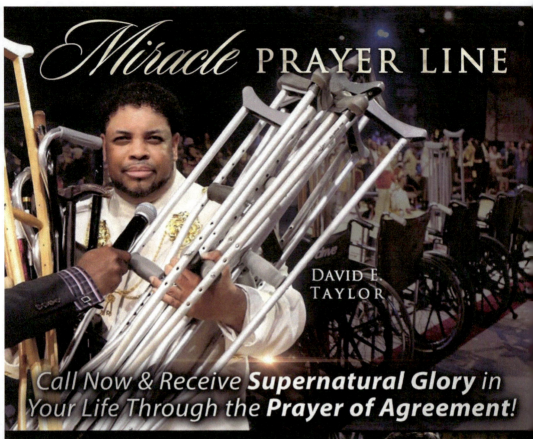

The Father Has Come *Down on Earth* to Visit Us!

"LO, I COME UNTO THEE IN A **THICK CLOUD**.." (EX. 19:9)
"FOR I WILL **APPEAR** IN THE **CLOUD**.." (LEV. 16:2)

AS SEEN ON FOX NEWS - CAPTURED LIVE ON VIDEO AS PROPHESIED BY DAVID E. TAYLOR

NEW BRUNSWICK, CANADA

The Ancient Biblical Move of Face-to-Face is *Back on the Earth* in the 21st Century with David E. Taylor

HASN'T BEEN SEEN FOR THOUSANDS OF YEARS!

Jesus first appeared face to face to David E. Taylor in a dream, when he was seventeen and a gangster on the streets. Jesus revealed Himself as the Savior and the Son of God. This appearance led to his conversion, much like Apostle Paul's on the road to Damascus.

Apostle Taylor fell in love with Jesus and radically pursued an intimate relationship with Him. This intense pursuit has increased over the years, and he continues to experience regular face to face visitations from Jesus (Many are detailed in his world-famous book, Face to Face Appearances from Jesus: The Ultimate Intimacy). Out of this face to face relationship, the ancient message of God's Kingdom, the one that Jesus taught his disciples two thousand years ago, was birthed and demonstrated. Since then, mass healings, miracles, deliverance, and divine restoration takes place, and the dead become resurrected! David quickly recognized the supernatural intimacy and power of God that was available to everyone who would believe. A deep compassion and desire came over David, and his prayer ever since has been for others to experience intimacy with the Lord through face to face visitations too.

In 2008, Jesus appeared to David E. Taylor in a dream, and commanded him to write a book that would shake the world. He said, "I want you to write a book on face to face appearances, and show my people by scripture how I did this throughout the Bible, and how I want all men to experience me like this. Use your life as a testimony that this relationship is possible to have with me in the twenty-first century. When you write this in a book, me and My Father will appear before whole regions in America and the nations and it will be captured on the news." The Lord Jesus also said to him, "I will draw near and appear to everyone who reads this book in dreams and visions." You will see in this article how this has already begun. When the book was released, Face to Face broke out, and now millions are experiencing intimacy with Jesus in their dreams and visions, resulting in global salvation.

People everywhere are giving their hearts to Jesus. This is happening throughout America and the world, just like Solomon experienced when the Lord appeared to him in a dream, "the LORD appeared to Solomon in a dream by night.." (1 Kings 3:4). Now, God is using this book as a tool to carry both His and His Son Jesus' words to highlight and restore the lost doctrine and New Testament promise of face to face intimacy that the church has overlooked for centuries!

"I will not leave you comfortless: I will come to you...he that loveth me shall be loved of my Father, and I will love him, and will manifest myself to him." (John 14:18,21)

The church has wrongly taught the message of seeing the Lord's face by misinterpreting such scriptures like, "Blessed are they that have not seen, and yet have believed" (John 20:29). In the New Testament, Jesus confirmed that He appeared face to face after His resurrection. In the above scripture, Jesus was not discounting the importance of making appearances to men, otherwise He wouldn't have appeared to Paul after He made this statement. But rather, He was rebuking the unbelief in the disciple Thomas who had walked with him face to face for three and a half years, and then had the audacity to challenge Him without faith.

Another scripture that people take out of context is when Jesus said, "if any man shall say unto you, Lo, here is Christ, or there; believe it not" (Mat.24:23). In these scriptures, Jesus was speaking about His second coming, and that before He comes, there will be many saying that He has already returned. This is not what David E. Taylor is proclaiming, instead, he is preaching about the Biblical manifestation that adheres to the very foundation of our Christian faith. Jesus not only died, but He rose again, and He still appears to His people face to face today! "Jesus Christ the same yesterday, and to day, and for ever" (Hebrews 13:8).

OREGON
"..FOR I WILL APPEAR IN THE CLOUD.." (LEV.16:2)

MISSOURI
"AND THE LORD CAME DOWN IN THE PILLAR OF THE CLOUD.." (NUM. 12:5)

MARYLAND
"...THE LORD **LOOKED**..THROUGH THE PILLAR..OF THE CLOUD..." (EX. 14:24)

The Latter Rain: How It All Started

In the year 2000, a visitation from the Lord happened that forever changed David's life. An eight-year old boy who was the son of a JMMI staff member, was taken to Heaven and spoke to Jesus. He received a message from Jesus to give to David. The message from Jesus was concerning the end-time move of God, known in the scriptures as the "Latter Rain". This message was so important to David, because he had been pursuing God about it for years.

In Heaven, the young boy saw a portal open up, showing him the future and what would take place. He gazed in amazement as he saw millions of people emptying out of their nations and coming to America because a massive move of God had hit! The little boy explained that he was at the Throne Room of God. David asked him if he had seen the Father, but the child said, "No, He wasn't on His throne." In amazement, David asked him, "Where was the Father?" The boy responded, "He was on the Earth working with you." The child went on to say, "This is the message Jesus sent me to give you."

The Father is the Latter Rain!

The scriptures are clear that God "came down'" from Heaven off His throne to work with Moses on the Earth to deliver His people! "And I am come down to deliver them" (Exodus 3:8). The child also gave David a message from Jesus, saying "Tell David that I am pleased with what he preaches because he doesn't preach what people want to hear, he preaches what I want to hear." David was shocked!

It took him six years to believe that the Father would come down again openly in the twenty-first century, making notable appearances in the cloud, working with him as He did with Moses and Jesus during their ministry on Earth. From the year 2000 up until about 2006, David proclaimed the message that the Father was going to come down on the Earth, although he wondered in his heart, "How could something of this magnitude happen?" He had always thought that the Latter Rain was

"*The Lord* Brought us out
with a mighty hand.. an Outstretched arm" *(Deut. 26:8)*

PORTUGAL   SCOTLAND   GEORGIA

CAPTURED LIVE ON VIDEO IN THE UKRAINE

Jesus & The Father
Working with David E. Taylor
on the Earth

"FOR THE EYES OF THE LORD RUN TO AND FRO THROUGHOUT THE WHOLE EARTH" - 2 CHRON. 16:9

Jesus coming and moving on the Earth. He also understood that this outpouring did not consist of another outpouring of the Holy Spirit, because the Holy Spirit was poured out already. When the visitation happened, the Holy Spirit began to connect all the scriptures to David's understanding, and it became clear to him that the Latter Rain is the Father Himself coming down on Earth! This will be an even greater outpouring! This is so much more than God just sending and pouring out His Spirit in the Earth. Father God Himself is coming off His throne and coming down to Earth to pour Himself out as the Latter Rain, in front of all men.

"Then shall we know, if we follow on to know the LORD.. he shall come unto us as the rain, as the latter and former rain unto the earth" (Hosea 6:3).

In Hebrew, the word "LORD" in this passage of scripture is "Jehovah" and it is referring to God the Father! The Father is the Latter Rain! The Father is the husbandman, He is a gardener! He is looking to harvest the crops (souls) of men on the Earth! He is coming down as the Latter Rain to prepare and water the people in order to bring in the end-time harvest of souls! "I am the true vine, and my Father is the husbandman" (John 15:1). The scriptures also bear witness in the epistle of James: "Behold, the husbandman waiteth for the precious fruit of the earth.. until he receive the early and latter rain" (James 5:7).

In 2006, Jesus appeared to David E. Taylor face to face while he was fasting and praying in the church. The Lord walked through the wall and spoke to him, promising that the message He gave him through the little boy was now starting! Jesus told David that He would not only use his life and ministry to appear to others, but that he had been given what Moses and what He Himself (Jesus) had in their life and ministry: the Father coming down in a cloud working notably in the eyesight of millions! This visitation gave David more confidence and faith!

After this Face to Face visitation from the Lord, it was just weeks later when the Father first came down as Jesus foretold to him. The Lord started telling David E. Taylor where He was going to show up and appear in the cloud, like He did with Moses when He appeared in the eyesight of three million Israelites on Mt. Sinai. God told Moses, "..the third day the LORD will come down in the sight of all the people upon mount Sinai" (Ex. 19:11). Since 2006, multiple appearances from the Lord have been and continue to be captured by the secular news media in every city that David E. Taylor proclaims the Lord will come down! God is notably doing it again in the twenty-first century with David E. Taylor, just as He came down notably in the cloud in both Moses' day and in the days of Jesus.

Face to Face in the 21st Century!

In Moses' time, the scriptures record that God came down with Moses in the cloud: "Lo, I come unto thee in a thick cloud."(Ex 19:9) "..the LORD came down in the pillar of the cloud.." (Num. 12:5) "..the LORD appeared in the tabernacle in a pillar of a cloud:" (Deut. 31:15) "..for I will appear in the cloud.." (Lev.16:2). The scriptures also record that God notably came down in the cloud in Jesus' time and spoke audibly in front of others! In Mark 9:7, the scriptures declare, "..there was a cloud that overshadowed them: and a voice came out of the cloud.." This is the ancient Biblical movement and ministry of Face to Face. God came down in the cloud with Moses and in the time of Jesus to bring deliverance to His people. In the Bible, God termed this action of coming down working with Moses on Earth in the cloud, talking to the children of Israel notably and openly, "Face to Face."

"The LORD talked with you face to face.."(-Deut. 5:4). Jesus told David E. Taylor that the Father was going to come down from Heaven to work with him in the Earth to bring deliverance to His people. God told Moses, "And I am come down to deliver them.." (Exodus 3:8). God is bringing deliverance! Souls are being saved, and thousands of miracles and healings are happening, including people being raised from the dead! Everywhere God sends David E. Taylor, drug rings and human slave trafficking principalities are being broken and obliterated on a massive scale; locally, regionally, nationally, and internationally! In America alone, hundreds of thousands of girls are sold into human slave trafficking every year from the ages of twelve to twenty-four. But God has come down, and is working on Earth with David E. Taylor to set His people free in our generation. Just as He was saying with Moses, "Let my people go", He is saying, "Let my girls go!" This deliverance is incredible!

The Father God, and Jesus His Son, are coming down on the Earth and appearing notably in the sight of millions, working with David E. Taylor in the twenty-first century, like they did in Biblical times, and it is being captured live on the news! This article illustrates just a few places (America, Canada, Scotland, Ukraine) that God the Father and Jesus said They would show up notably with David E. Taylor, and it happened! This is amazing! As of this time, the LORD has shown up in over 20 places! To see more places where the LORD has appeared and to read the rest of this article about the new Move of God on the scene, visit his website!

MONTANA
KAZAKHSTAN
CHICAGO, ILLINOIS
LONDON, ENGLAND
MEMPHIS, TENNESSEE

For more information about David E. Taylor, to contact the author for speaking engagements, or for additional copies of this book and other book titles as well as a complete list of all products, visit: www.kingdomofgodglobalchurch.org
or call 1-877-THE-GLORY

Send your requests to:
Kingdom of God Global Church
20320 Superior Rd
Taylor, MI 48180

"The Kingdom of God is the Message, Face to Face is the Move!"